Liverpool Waif

Liverpool Waif

by

Bob Houghton

Print Origination (NW) Ltd
Formby Business Park
Formby, Liverpool L37 8EG

ISBN 0 903348 33 0

First Published in 1992 by
Print Origination (NW) Ltd
Formby Business Park
Formby, Liverpool L37 8EG

Typeset in 10pt Rockwell by
Print Origination (NW) Ltd, Formby, Liverpool L37 8EG
Printed and bound in Britain by Courier International Ltd., East Kilbride

Dedication

I dedicate this book to all the Burscough Boatmen past and present, the majority of whom are related to me by inter-marriage.

A special dedication to Tom and Ann Bowen who now lie at well earned rest in the small churchyard of Christchurch Douglas on Parbold Hill.

To my wife Eunice, my gratitude and thanks for her encouragement which made me write this story.

The author Bob Houghton in centre with his two brothers c. 1930

Chapter One

Early Days of the family

In 1882 Henry Houghton, my paternal grandfather, was a 30-year-old Canadian mariner working as a ships bosun on a sailing ship owned by the then Pappayanni Line, whose registered offices were in Fenwick Street, Liverpool. Their ships sailed between Montreal and Liverpool.

In that same year he met and married a young Irish girl, Mary Ann Bell who at 23 was seven years his junior. Her family originated from Dublin and emigrated to England at a time when there was a mass exodus due to lack of employment combined with the failure of the potato crop causing widespread famine throughout the country.

She was a Roman Catholic; Henry was an Anglican, and on March 8th 1882 they were married in the Protestant church of St Alban's in Bevington Hill, Bevington Bush, Liverpool.

Two months after the marriage Henry sailed back to Canada, leaving behind him his now-pregnant bride with definate instructions regarding the child should it prove to be a boy. On December 17th that year, while Henry was still away at sea, Mary gave birth to the son they both wanted. In accordance with one of her husband's wishes, she christened him Richard after Henry's father but she failed to observe the second condition her husband had laid down namely to christening in the Anglican Church.

Henry must have been proud of his father who had been a ships carpenter in Montreal, involved in the actual building of new vessels from oak rather than just their subsequent repair.

Henry arrived back at the family home in Bond Street, off Vauxhall Road, in March 1883 and looked forward eagerly to seeing his son for the first time. His pleasure was dulled, however, when he discovered that the child had been baptized a Roman Catholic, so, nothing daunted, the proud father took his baby son along to the Anglican church where he and his wife had been married and insisted on his being baptized again, this time into the Church of England.

Unlike my Irish grandmother, Henry Houghton could read and write. He went to sea once more but was destined never to return to his baby son and young wife in Liverpool. In November 1883 he was found drowned in Montreal harbour, where his ship was berthed. His personal possessions were returned to Liverpool, together with the name plate from his coffin lid, so my grandfather is buried in his native Canada, in Montreal, and my father, Richard, was to grow up never to know him. Elder members of my family recalled that the name Houghton had been mispelt Haughton.

In 1900 the Pappayanni shipping line, which was then owned by four Greek brothers, was taken over by the growing Harrison Line.

My dad, during his early years, was brought up in the Vauxhall Road area of Liverpool, near to the docks. The district was dominated by the giant Tate & Lyle sugar refinery, which was built straddling both sides of the Leeds and Liverpool Canal, between Scotland Road and the Dock Road.

A lot of time, as a small boy, he was left to fend for himself. His widowed mother spent most of her time in one or other of the numerous public houses and grog shops that abounded in the vicinity of Scotland Road. He was to grow up illiterate and, like his mother, he was never sent to school, perhaps one of the reasons was because in those days, before the turn of the century, it wasn't compulsory, and parents had to pay tuppence (two pence) a week to the newly-formed Education Authorities, towards the cost.

Another reason for her not sending my father to school could have been because as she herself could neither read or write, she may well have thought, in her ignorance, it was neither necessary or advantageous for him to attend.

Bargees who worked the wide boats (sadly long since gone) on the Leeds and Liverpool Canal, remembered my father as a small boy in the 1890s, sitting on the canal's edge, paddling his feet in the water and swimming in the *cut* (canal) itself, along with other little urchins. Most of them swam in the *nuddy* (naked). None of them could have afforded a swimming costume or thought one necessary anyhow.

Water was used in the Tate & Lyle factory for boiling sugar cane and

Tate & Lyle's unloading berths, Liverpool kids used to swim in the warm water here, 1950

was discharged into the canal by outlet pipes, making the canal warm, especially between Burlington Street and Chisenhale Street bridges, a distance of approximately a hundred yards. It was a favourite rendez-vous for the poor bare-footed ill-clad lads who lived in the neighbour-hood, it was the only warm bath they knew. There were no bathrooms in the houses they lived in, the best they could hope for was the use of a long tin bath which hung up on a nail in the back yard when not in use.

About 1900, and six years after becoming a widow, my grandmother went to live *over the brush* (unmarried) with a widower named Walter Reynolds. He had a son named Walter who was the same age as my father. Walter senior was a bargee on the canal and lived in a small house in a row that was adjacent to the canal side. It was in a part of the original Bootle known as Bootle Village. This illicit union lasted for 19 years, until my grandmother died in 1919. She is buried in the Roman Catholic Cemetery at Ford, a mile or so north of Bootle Village. Walter Reynolds, her common law husband, was later buried amongst the Protestants in Bootle Borough Cemetery.

My dad and young Walter Reynolds were brought up together for 19 years, and they always referred to each other as *our Walter* and *our Dick* as though they were natural brothers. Not surprisingly, they both became boatmen on the canal and were known as Dick and Walter *Ranty*.

My dad started his working life in 1890 when he was 8 years old. He commenced by helping some of the hundreds of bargees who worked and lived on the boats in those days. The majority of them were from up country (places north of Liverpool) on the canal route. For payment of pennies or sometimes just food, like a jam butty, he started to help them with the many chores needed to be carried out after each trip. Boats needed their holds cleaned and brushed and decks washed after discharging coal at Tate & Lyles, or the Athol Street Gas Works. Boatmen needed to replenish the fresh water casks kept on top of the stern end deck where the *living in* cabin was situated before setting off back to the Wigan Coalfields. The water had to be carried in buckets from the nearest tap, probably the one in the stable yard. Boat horses required their stable stalls mucked out every day, especially when it was time to depart, so as to leave them clean and ready for the next occupant.

The most favoured stables in the area was Dick Snaylam's yard, situated on the corner of Vauxhall Road and Lightbody Street. The majority of boat horses were accommodated there for the one or two days necessary. The charge in the late 1930s was one shilling and six pence for each, or part of, a twenty-four hour stay, with clean straw bedding provided.

Bread and provisions had to be got in, for both man and beast, the bread from the many small shops in Vauxhall Road, Scotland Road, or from Paddys Market in Cazeneu Street, and the oats for the horses from perhaps Musker's provender stores in Strand Road, Bootle, or from one of the many stores that have long since gone.

At times a new half inch in diameter cotton tow rope would be required from a ships chandlers on the Dock Road. There were many and varied jobs to be performed; and that's how my father was introduced to what Liverpool people referred to as the *flatties*. The name had derived from the fact that the holds of the barges had flat bottoms!

Most boatmen on the canal qualified, sooner or later, for a nick-name, after becoming a member of what was a very close fraternity. It was acquired by an individual having a certain characteristic, a way of life, or something which he might have once said or done. Once bestowed it remained with them for the rest of their lives.

No-one seems to know why the Reynolds family were always called

Linacre Village, 1890.

the *Rantys*, someone had suggested it was because they were always ranting and raving in pubs. Although my dad was illiterate, he was never short of words, and could always be heard above every other drinker in a public bar. I suppose he could be aptly termed a *loud mouth*, but in spite of all his failings and handicaps, he had a wonderful sense of humour. He was funny even though most times he didn't realize it.

He always judged the class of a pub by the fact of whether it had sawdust on the floor, and spittoons. If it did not, it was, in his estimation, a pub of poor class.

At the age of 17 he was a fully qualified barge captain, navigating a horse-drawn boat between Liverpool and Wigan. A stark contrast to the occupation of his Canadian father who had sailed the Atlantic Ocean for his living.

On March 6th 1905 my father married my mother in St Matthew's Church, Bootle. He was 23 and she 19.

My mother's maiden name was Ann Cheetham. She met my father when her family went to live in New Street, in what was known then as Bootle-Cum- Linacre. They came from Cinders Lane Burscough Town in the country parish of Lathom near Ormskirk Lancashire, some 20 miles from Bootle as the canal flows, or 14 miles via the public highway.

There was a total of eight in the Cheetham family, my mother's parents Henry and Jane Cheetham, my mother, her four sisters and

one brother. The Cheethams were also a boating family as a consequence, when they moved house, all their belongings and chattels were
transported by my father's canal boat from Burscough Canal Bridge to
Linacre Lane Canal Bridge Bootle. That's how my dad met my mother he
was the captain of the boat.

My maternal grandfather Henry Cheetham was born at Halsall West
Lancashire, on the 26th of December 1845, and his father, John
Cheetham, who was also a boatman, worked on the canal very shortly
after it was opened in 1770.

Grandfather Henry Cheetham married my grandmother in Liverpool
Parish Church on the 23rd of October 1884. At that time my granny, (nee
Jane Culshaw) was a 23 year old spinster with an 18 month old baby girl
named Mary Elizabeth, who was born in a canalside cottage called the
Bog Houses near New Lane, Burscough. Henry was a 38 year old
widower, who had two daughters from his first marriage. He died of
General Paralysis in the Union Workhouse Ormskirk on the 14th of May
1909. The name of the informant of his death was the Master of the
Workhouse a Mr A. H. Whitaker Esq.

On my parents' marriage certificate, my father's name was written as
Aughton instead of Houghton, and of course it remains that way in
records today. I can only assume that when the vicar officiating at their
wedding asked my father his name, although he of course was able to
pronounce it, he was not able to spell it out to him. The vicar perhaps
thinking of Aughton Church, a well-known landmark 8 miles from
Bootle, guessed incorrectly and spelt the name thus so. The marriage
certificate therefore contains a wrongly spelt name and two X's (Their
Mark) as signatures.

My happy days at home

I was born at the family home 149 Litherland Road, on February 11th
1924. Although the official postal address is Bootle Lancashire. The
once independent County Borough is more inclined to be thought of
as a suburb of the great Port of Liverpool. In no way could you
identify Liverpool people as being Lancastrians. Scousers are best
known for their distinctive Southern Irish connection, and inherited half
Irish accent, rather than a Lancastrian identity. A Yorkshireman is a
Yorkshireman, no matter which part of the county he comes from not so,
I imagine is a Lancastrian.

To hear the dulcet tones of the Lancashire dialect being spoken you
only have to go a short distance north of Bootle, to Ormskirk Market

Brothers George (left) and Richard (right) with me, wearing the second hand suits our father purchased when left £100 in the will of bargeowner and employer John Parke.

Town, or east to Prescot or St Helens.

I spent the first ten years of my life in cobble-stoned, gas- lit, Litherland Road. It is still a road that for most of its one-mile length has houses on the west side, and a 12 feet high gas works wall on the east side. It runs north to south parallel to the 16 miles of Dock Road, a half mile away to the west. The Docks themselves, once a hive of activity, are now sadly laying mostly derelict and silent.

The front doors of the 1850-built Litherland Road houses lead straight out on to the pavement. The large low-silled window at the side of each door was known as the parlour window. At our house, the parlour was occupied by my grandmother Cheetham, who lived and slept there. My immediate family lived in the rear of the house, and slept in the three upstairs bedrooms.

When I was born the family consisted of my father and mother, three surviving brothers, and one sister. The eldest of the family was my big brother Henry, named after the found drowned Canadian grandfather Houghton. Brother Henry was 18 years old when I was born, the next oldest was Jane Elizabeth 14, Richard 10, and George 4½. My dad was 42 at the time of my arrival, and my mother 38.

Grandmother Cheetham, 1928.

Besides being a boatman, my dad was also a coal heaver, before the days of mechanisation, and the introduction of steam cranes and grabs, boats on the canal had their 60-70 tonnes of coal discharged by hand. This was done with spades, wheel-barrows, planks to wheel them on, and human muscle. When he was not engaged in that very physical activity, he was navigating a horse-drawn boat along lengths of the canal.

What I remember from my childhood days about the house on Litherland Road in the 1930s, was first, the hallway which we called the lobby this led from the front door to the back of the house. The first door on the left along the lobby going in was grannies parlour, the second led into the family living room. This room contained a window which looked out onto the back yard, and in front of the window was a table from which we sat to eat all our meals. It was always covered with a flowery patterned oilcloth, and around it were five chairs, all different shapes and sizes, each bought second hand as the family increased.

There was a sideboard with cupboards and two top drawers, in which all the important documents were kept, such as life insurance weekly payment books, and all other credit repayment books. Amongst them also would be a pawn ticket or two, awaiting better financial times, and put there, not only for safe keeping, but to keep tally on renewal dates, to make sure the articles pledged were not forfeited and sold by the pawnbroker.

We had a five barred, black leaded cast iron fire-grate, with a shiny steel oven door on one side; on the top bar, a 'looby' was attached, to stand a large cast iron kettle and pans on. Over the fire-grate was a mantlepiece, this was adorned with a hanging length of green tassled velvet. Identical ornamental pottery dogs stood at each end, and in the centre was the wind-up clock. This was wound, and had its alarm set every night by my father before he took it upstairs to bed with him.

On the walls of the living room there were two prints in frames, one was of a silk suited boy, belonging to another century, standing in front of a table behind which sat three of his elders, they were attired in feather plumed hats and pantaloons. the Caption at the bottom of the picture read 'When Did You Last See Your Father?'

On the opposite wall was a picture of a white horse, a mare with its brown foal. The caption to this was: 'Mother And Son.' The living room floor was of red stone square quarry tiles, and in one corner were the wooden stairs that led up to the three unheated bedrooms.

Although the two downstairs rooms; the parlour and the living room, had gas mantle lighting, the bedrooms did not have any no lighting at all. The rooms were illuminated by carrying a lighted candle into them, stuck to a saucer by its own wax.

I remember too, the three removable iron shelves inside the fire-grate oven. On a cold winter's night, these shelves, when warm, were wrapped in old pieces of blanket, carried upstairs and placed between the bedclothes to warm the bed prior to getting into it.

At rear of the houses there was a backyard, at the end of which the only toilet of the house was situated. This was the reason why chamber pots, or *poes* as we called them, were kept under the bed. They helped prevent you catching pneumonia by having to get up out of a warm bed, and go downstairs into the yard on a freezing night, to answer the call of nature.

At the bottom of the yard, inserted into the wall, was a square pull-down metal rubbish receptacle for household refuse. which were known as *muck middens*. A wooden back door in the wall led out into the entry or the *jigger*, which was about 2 metres wide running along the back of all the houses in the street with an exit at each end. The streets around about all had rural sounding names like Ash, Beech, Cedar, Elm and Oak, etc. In reality there wasn't a tree or a blade of grass to be seen. Even in the 1930s the area was a depressing sight, and yet today, these same houses still remain, and are lived in.

I was born into a family dogged by ill-luck, before I was born a brother and a sister had died in tragic circumstances. It wasn't until I was 14 years old, after returning to Bootle, after my enforced incarcerated in the home for waifs and strays, that my sister Jane, (Once Mammy Janie) enlightened me about some of the facts concerning the family's history.

Bootle-cum-Linacre Gas Works, Bootle.

She told me a brother named John had worked in a railway coal sidings, filling coal into 1 cwt bags from railway wagons for domestic house delivery. Whilst doing so he overtasked himself, causing internal injuries, which had a fatal result he died in Walton Hospital at 17 years of age. A few weeks later a sister, Mary Ann, named after my dad's mother, was run over by a steam driven lorry, right opposite her own front door. The lorry came over and down the cobblestoned Litherland Road Canal Bridge, which was only 20 yards south of the door. Mary Ann had been playing ball with a little friend in the lobby with the front door wide open when, child-like, she ran out into the road to retrieve the ball they had been playing with; she ran straight into the path of the lorry, giving the driver no chance of avoiding her.

At the time of the accident my father was working less than a quarter of a mile from the bridge, along the canal towpath. He was shovelling out a barge load of coal at Bootle Gas Works when a policeman walked along the canal bank and broke the news to him. I was told how my mother picked Mary Ann up from the roadway and carried her back into the house. Although there was no obvious signs of injury she died in my mother's arms before the ambulance arrived, she was 3 years old.

Sadness enters my life

I had always assumed that I was the last born, and the baby of the family, being only 23 months old when my mother died I was therefore surprised to learn that when I was 18 months old another brother, John Fred, was born. He was so named to replace John sadly, he died of meningitis in Alder Hey Childrens Hospital when only 4 months old. My mother died shortly afterwards no doubt of a broken heart just five days before her 40th birthday.

After my mother's death, sister Jane took over the role of mother-cum-housekeeper, she was 16 and I was approaching my second birthday, 'Mammie Janie' reared me until I was 10.

One of my earliest and most vivid memories was the death of my granny Cheetham. She died 4 years after my mother in 1930, an occasion which has remained in my memory to this day. Her body was laid out in her own parlour and as she was a woman of large proportions a specially erected trestle table was used.

At the time I was told by Janie, 'not to go into the parlour while Gran was resting'. Lots of people came to the house and were shown into the parlour to see her. I remember how well I did financially, with quite a number of the visitors giving me pennies. I also remember thinking 'If Gran died every day, I'd have lots of money!'

Being a small boy however, curiosity got the better of me and when I thought no-one was about, I opened the parlour door and peered in to see my granny laying there. It was the first time I'd looked on death and I found it strange and frightening. Seeing her in the middle of the room, with a white sheet covering all but her face, I could not comprehend that she would never move anymore, or that she would never again sit at the front door on a nice day, knitting for hours on end as she often did, or ever speak to me from now on. As I looked at her, so still and so quiet, I felt sure if I shouted her name she would surely answer me, as she had always done in the past. Before any sound passed my lips, I was bade by Janie to come away and close the door.

On the day of her funeral I watched as the motor car hearse, and the one car behind, stopped outside our front door. Quite a number of our neighbours had gathered on the pavement, both sides of the door, awaiting their arrival.

There were a number of people inside the house, including big brother Henry and he seemed to be in charge of the proceedings. My dad was present also; it was the first time I'd seen him dressed in a suit of clothes with a collar and tie. The suit had to be given back the next

Canal families and cottages, Newburgh ('Newbruff'), Parbold, 1920.

day to a neighbour from whom it had been borrowed.

In the 1930s the motor car was still a comparatively new phenomenon. In my short life I'd often seen the horse-drawn corteges passing along the cobbled streets of Bootle. I can still picture the square window framed hearses with their large polished wooden wheels and shining hub caps, and in my mind's eye I can see the pairs of Belgian jet black horses, with black plumes on top of their headgear, pulling the carriages. There were always two men seated on top of the hearse, one of them holding the reins, controlling the horses. They wore tall round top hats and nearly always had a rug over their knees to keep their legs warm.

The reason why Granny Cheetham was being taken away by motor car, and not by horses, was because it had been her wish that her last resting place should be where she had grown up as a young girl, and the place her own parents lay buried. This was in St John's Churchyard, Burscough Town and as it was a 14 mile journey it was just a bit too far for the horses to travel from Bootle and return the same day. I watched with sadness as my Granny was driven away from her parlour and my life forever.

A few weeks after the funeral the empty parlour was rented to a retired bargee. His name was Dick Jackson he was a widower who my dad had known for years and, like himself, was a regular drinker in one of the four public houses on Litherland Road Bootle Village. The one they most frequented was the Laburnum Hotel, always referred to as *The Blobber* as it is to this day.

Chapter Two

The Lodger

Dick Jackson had mentioned to my dad that he was looking for fresh digs, and so he was offered the front parlour as a bed-sitter for half-crown a week (12½p), self catering with the use of the two-ringed gas stand in the back kitchen for cooking.

In those days, if there was a room to spare, it would be rented out to a lodger as a means of supplementing a low income. Landlords didn't bother about such practices of sub-letting or possibly they never became aware of it.

It transpired if you went back far enough into Dick Jackson's genealogy, he was a distant relation of my mother and the Cheethams. Canal boatmen did a lot of inter-marrying, it was a frequent occurrence for first cousins to marry which could have been one of the reasons why quite a few bargees finished their days in one of the workhouses or lunatic asylums, before they were called mental homes many of which served both purposes. It is said inter-breeding may be a contributory factor in causing insanity.

Old Dick Jackson was turned 70 when he came to live at our house he had qualified for the state pension of 10 shillings a week. He too had spent his working life on the Leeds and Liverpool Canal, but he still hadn't finished working. He was now a night watchman, employed by the local Electricity Board. It was described as a part-time job, although he had to 'watch' for 50 hours a week. You could say he received part-time wages for doing the work. His hours were from 8 pm to 6 am, 5 nights a week, Monday to Friday, and his rates of pay were sixpence (2½p) an hour—one pound twenty five pence a week.

Tom Bowen ('Old Shiney') being pulled through Barnoldswick by 'Ben', 1924.

In the early 1930s the local electricity works had their yard and offices in Hawthorne Road, next to the gas works. It was a 10 minute walk from our house. In the yard were kept all the motor vehicles, some horse and carts, stables and giant bobbins of electric cable.

Electricity was beginning to replace a lot of the gas appliances at the time. When all the workmen had gone home for the day, and the gates to the yard had been closed and locked for the night, it was Dick Jackson's job to see no-one climbed over the wall in the night to break in.

Just inside the green wooden double gates stood a watchman's hut. It was a structure of about 7 ft high, 4 ft wide and 4 ft deep. Inside was a bench across its width to sit on. Standing in front of the hut was a three-legged coke burning brazier, which stopped 'old Dick' from freezing to death in the early hours of a winter's morning. The fire also served as a means to make toasted bread and boil the water in his tea can, into which he would empty a mixture of loose tea, sugar, and condensed milk, this was wrapped in greaseproof paper and brought from home. The sticky ball was put in the can and stirred when the water had boiled.

When Dick the watchman had lived in our parlour for a short time, I adopted him as my new grandad. I was 7 years old when I was given the job of taking his supper to him on daylight summer evenings. It was sister Jane who got grandad's supper ready for about 9 pm. I would walk the short distance via Marsh Lane Canal Bridge carrying a china basin always wrapped in a red neckerchief with white spots, knotted at the top to make a handle, with which to carry it upright so as not to spill the contents.

In the basin would be perhaps a hot rabbit broth or pea soup, to warm grandad Jackson and keep out the cold night air.

When I arrived at the works, I would rattle the small wicket gate and shout until grandad opened it. Very often he would ask me to sit in the hut in front of the fire and keep guard, while he nipped along to the Albion Public House on Hawthorne Road, for a quick pint of 5 penny (2p) beer then return to eat his supper. He would be gone for about 20 minutes. I used to sit with him for a while as he ate to relieve some of the boredom and loneliness of his 10 hour shifts. As a reward, every Saturday, he gave me three pennies.

It was in 1933 when I was nine that my grandad Jackson died. Besides the occasion being another sad loss to me, it was also a financial one. Where now was I to get my money to enable me to see the children's Saturday afternoon matinee performances at the cinema?

My Business Venture

I was attending Hawthorne Road Council School, but I never did like going to school very much and on many occasions, when I was supposed to be in the classroom I was not. Sister Jane used to take me in the mornings for 9 am but if it was a nice dry sunny day, at the first opportunity, like the mid-morning playtime break. I would walk out of the open gates and make my way down to the Dock Road to watch all the hustle and bustle that went on there. I loved to see the beautiful cart horses in their hundreds, pulling the heavy loads of merchandise, being taken to the scores of ships berthed in the docks, or being taken from them to the giant warehouses for storage and distribution. I loved to read the strange sounding destinations stencilled on the wooden barrels and crates which were bound for the different countries that made up the then British Empire.

Often you saw sparks coming from both the horses metal shoes and from the solid steel-rimmed wheels of the carts as they grated on the cobblestoned roads.

The bows of the merchant ships came close up to the main road, towering over everything except the multi-storey high warehouses.

The names of the many vessels were displayed on their bows, some-

Me with Mrs Yates (owner of sweet shop next door) and her daughter Lydia, 1928.

times in the English language, or the Roman type of lettering, but some would be in the Chinese or Japanese style of writing.

On my walks I was always emulating the thousands of pigeons and seagulls flying around by picking up Indian corn that had fallen from a split bag on a cart and eating the seeds.

When I'd walked as far as the Pier Head and came in sight of the Liver Birds perched on top of the Liver Buildings, and saw the Ferry Boats crossing the River Mersey, it was my cue to turn around and head back towards Bootle. For me, beyond the Pier Head was strange territory; It was the commencement of the South End of Liverpool, and I belonged to the North. The Liver Buildings themselves denoted a North / South divide, and I never ventured beyond it; besides it was a 3-mile walk back to Bootle from there and I had to time it to arrive home at 4 pm. as if I'd been to school and had just come from there.

I liked to walk abreast of the lovely horses as they were pulling the heavy loads. I admired the different coloured coats, with their individual markings and of course their strength. When they were stationary at the roadside, I had the uncontrollable urge to go up to them and stroke their spongy noses. Invariably at these times it wasn't always possible because their faces were half covered by nose bags strapped on them, as they ate their provender. The drovers or carters as they were better known, would be in one of the many *cocoa rooms* also having something to eat. They called it having their *scoff* in Liverpool jargon.

It was whilst walking along the road one day that I conceived the idea that the vast amounts of manure deposited on the roads could have a value for use on gardens or allotments. As I gave the idea more thought, the first problem I had to solve was the transportation of the 'free for the taking' commodity to potential customers, this was soon resolved when I arrived home. Next door to where we lived at 147 Litherland Road, was a small general shop, it was run by Miss Lydia Yates who managed it on behalf of her aged parents who she lived with on the premises. They too had originated from the country, from Ormskirk, Mr Yates was a retired carter.

I asked Lydia if she had an empty wooden box she could let me have, (without charge of course). She gave me one that had contained Sunlight Soap. I then cadged a pair of wheels on an axle discarded from an old perambulator. With two pieces of wood, to serve as shafts, and a little help from brother George using a saw and a few nails a small cart was knocked together. I was now ready to enter into business as a purveyor of fresh horse manure.

I was excited and enthusiastic about my venture into the world of commerce, Sister Jane warned me to use caution while I was on the Dock Roads. At least the traffic didn't move as fast as it does today.

One Saturday morning, pushing the cart armed with the small household shovel, I started off for the gathering fields. When I arrived, the mounds of gold were abundant, I filled the cart within half an hour. Retracing my way back home, I showed off the garden fertilizer to the family before making my way to where I thought I could sell it. Sister Jane was more interested in the whereabouts of the small shovel, normally used for putting coal on our fire.

There was no possibility of selling the manure in the neighbourhood of Litherland Road, the only semblance of a garden you saw near our house was perhaps a potted aspidistra in a front parlour window.

After my dinner (lunch) I pushed the cart the short distance to the more select residential area of Southport Road, where a lot of the business and professional people of Bootle lived. They were the middle class residents of Bootle, the remainder being out of work working class.

These houses were privately owned and had gardens both back and front. At the first posh house I approached, feeling a little sheepish and apprehensive, I walked up the path to the front door; it had one of the new type of bells that worked by electricity. I left the cart heaped with muck on the pavement not daring to show it, fearing the mere sight of it might give offence.

'The Liverpool Waif' aged 6, by Gasworks wall, Litherland Road, Bootle, 1930.

I rang the highly polished bell hoping to make a sale and not to get a shock from the new-fangled bell. A rather large lady opened the door which increased my nervousness, I would have preferred it had been a man. It didn't seem to be the best of good manners to ask a lady of quality if she wanted to buy a load of horse muck even though I called it manure.

The lady, on seeing my small ragged figure standing at her door, was about to say 'No' even before I stated my reason for ringing her bell. With a quick change of mind, I think more out of curiosity than courtesy, she hesitated, and listened to my utterings of: 'Want to buy some garden manure Misses?' She replied: 'No Thank you, and close the gate on your way out'. With that last remark she shut the door.

While I was having some difficulty with the lock on the gate I could see her watching me from a front window. Suddenly the front door opened again, I thought at first she was going to set the dog, or her husband, on to me as a warning not to call anymore, but instead she shouted, 'Let me see it,' meaning, of course, the natural soil stimulant.

In thinking of the financial side of my undertaking, I calculated that half the load was worth threepence, and the whole box full, scraped clean, sixpence.

She came to the gate to see my wares and said, 'How much is it?' With a sound, reminiscent of a young frog, coming from my vocal cords, I replied: 'Sixpence Misses'. She said: 'Wheel it around the back'. With a feeling of failure turned into sudden success, I pushed the cart up the driveway and through a side gate, into her back garden.

She indicated the spot where she wanted the manure dumped. I tipped up the cart and, workman like, scraped the remnants from the box with my shovel. When the sixpenny piece was put into my hand, she asked where I lived. When I told her, she said 'Will you be having any more". I replied: 'Yes Mrs'. She then asked me to call the following Saturday with another cart load. I pushed the empty cart home feeling very pleased with myself, and kept feeling in my trouser pocket to make sure the silver sixpence was still safe in my possession.

A few more Saturdays went by with my continuing to collect manure from the roads, and unwittingly helping to keep them a little cleaner, brought me cash rewards and I developed a taste for the good life. At 9 years of age and a country in deep depression, I for one had plenty of work to do, and always had coppers in my pocket.

I found this latest way of making money a lot easier than dragging a piece of sleeper from the railway sidings, (under cover of darkness) then having to saw it into blocks with a saw that was badly in need of sharpening, before chopping it into sticks to bundle; carrying the bundles from door to door selling them as firewood to start coal fires. It was a lot less strenuous and more expeditious.

Chapter Three

A Taste of The Good Life

I could read and write enough to scan the two Liverpool evening newspapers, the *Liverpool Echo* and the *Evening Express* each listing what was now being screened on the picture houses and music halls, and who was appearing on the live stage. There were always lots of different films including musicals, comedies, cowboy pictures, and gangster films to choose from. There were singers of great stature such as Richard Tauber singing 'You Are My Hearts Delight', Allan Jones (Donkey Serenade), Nelson Eddy and Jeanette McDonald.

The current crop of cowboys of the day were Ken Maynard, Tom Mix, Hoot Gibson, William Boyd (Hopalong Cassidy) and Gary Cooper. The funny men were Stan Laurel and Oliver Hardy, Harold Lloyd, Buster Keaton and Charlie Chaplin.

Most of the dramatic actors were British: Robert Donat in such films as 'Goodbye Mr Chips' and 'The Count of Monte Cristo'. Other great actors were C. Aubrey Smith, Basil Rathbone, Claude Rains, George Arliss, and not forgetting Charles Laughton in 'Mutiny on The Bounty', with Clarke Gable as Fletcher Christian.

The ultra gangster was Edward G. Robinson in films like 'Little Caesar'. We loved them all.

The two theatres nearest to our house were the *Metropole* on Stanley Road Bootle, and the *Rotunda* by Scotland Road Kirkdale. On the stage frequently could be seen the famous Scottish comedian and singer of Scottish songs Harry Lauder, later to become Sir Harry, Hetty King, Bertha Wilmot, or the Lancashire comedians Frank Randle, George Formby, and Liverpool's own Robb Wilton. Sadly they've all gone, the singers, actors, comedians, the theatres, and the picture houses.

The Metropole Theatre, Bootle.

A large part of my 'good' life was spent in the music halls and the picture houses. An added treat, before going in was to buy a newspaper full of 'fades'. For a penny you could by them from most fruit shops. They were different kinds of fruit that was beginning to go bad. You just simply cut out the rotting part, and consumed the remainder. It was convenient to have a small pen-knife for such operations otherwise it meant using your fingers, to scoop away the rotten parts.

After the shows and performances were over, it was time for a visit to the *chippy*, for a tupenny mix. This was a small piece of fish, a few chips, a dessert spoonful of peas, and one scollop. It was after some of this *high living*, that had become a habit, my thoughts would turn to going home.

When I arrived back home after one of these jaunts my sister Jane would be waiting sometimes almost at the point of calling the police to report me as a missing person. She wanted to know where I'd been since leaving home that morning at about 8.45, to go to school. On certain days she would guess I hadn't been to school at all, but had been out with the cart on the roads and spending the proceeds. My total absence from home since leaving in the mornings often amounted to 11 or 12 hours. She used to warn me that if I didn't mend my ways I would be taken away for *sagging* (being absent) school. It was a warning I did not heed until it was too late.

What with collecting horse droppings, eating in cocoa rooms on the Dock Road through the day, and visits to the halls of entertainment in the evenings, I hardly had time to go home except to sleep.

The Wind of Change

By now the truant officer from Bootle Town Hall was making frequent visits to our house, wanting to know the reason why I was absent from school on so many occasions.

In the meantime, big brother Henry got married and left home. I was told he went to live somewhere near to Walton Prison. I didn't see him again until years later.

Brother George went to live with Henry my father was travelling the lengths of the canal and we seldom saw him. Jane was having difficulty contacting him to get money with which to buy food and to pay the rent of the house.

Brother Richard was in Alder Hey Children's Hospital with a damaged hip bone, sustained while playing in a stable yard. The condition of Osteomyelitis set into the injury, and he remained in the hospital for 5 years having to undergo numerous operations. Penicillin would have made a great contribution towards his treatment, but it had not yet been discovered.

Late in 1933 George left school and started his first job. It was with a small Bootle company called *Radio Zip*. He was employed to ride a pedal tricycle with a box attached to the front similar to a Walls *Stop Me and Buy One* ice cream cycle. His job was to call on private households to exchange their wet accumulators (batteries) for re-charged ones. These were the means of powering wireless sets in those days prior to electricity to get reception from them.

I remember George wore a peaked cap and a leather cash bag over one shoulder and collected money from each of the households he called on.

One day in May 1934 before I realized what was happening my little world came crashing down around me. We had to leave the family house at 149 Litherland Road because of non-payment of the rent.

My sister Jane who had looked after me since I was less than two years old got married and went to live in lodgings.

I was taken to a strange house in Norris Green by a man from Bootle Town Hall where I was handed over to a middle aged couple they were

My sister 'Mamie' (Janie) at sweet 17, 1927.

members of the Salvation Army. I was told they were to be my foster parents. They had no children of their own.

It seemed as though I was having a nightmare and nothing would induce me to stay with these strangers not all the kind words, or the tea and cakes. I just wanted to be back to the familiar surroundings of Bootle Village and the smell of the gas works, and Williams Toffee Factory.

Within a matter of only hours after being lodged at Norris Green, I ran away and walked the three miles back to Bootle. When I arrived at our house to my utter dismay, it was empty. On the windows, where once my grannie's curtains used to hang, newspapers had been put up. In desperation I thought of my Aunt Alice. I didn't know the addresses of my sister or brother Henry, but I knew Aunt Alice lived by the seashore in Waterloo a couple of miles north of Bootle. I had been taken there on a number of occasions by Janie. The reason for our visit had been to borrow money to buy food. Aunt Alice was one of my mother's younger sisters and a widow from the First World War her husband was killed in France on the Somme in 1917. She was a State Registered Nurse and was known locally as Nurse Burns.

When I think now of how Mammie Janie must have worked just to keep body and soul together approaching different people for money and old clothes it was no wonder she got fed up with it all and got married.

I also remember being taken by her to a place called the Unemployment Assistance Board Offices, or the U.A.B. for short. The office was in a small cul-de-sac called Cyprus Grove, in Cyprus Road, which was off Marsh Lane. I used to think it had been situated in such a place so it couldn't be found too easily.

Jane and I had to wait for hours before being interviewed in a small inner office. If the powers that were in charge came to the conclusion that you qualified for assistance, you would be given a voucher with which to buy food. These vouchers were of three values, and came in three colours; a green one was worth £1, blue ten shillings (50p), and red five shillings (25p). It was said in Bootle those days among the poor that to qualify for a £1 voucher, you had to be in possession of a letter from either God, or the Pope in Rome, with your application. No-one was given anything until they fulfilled all the necessary conditions. For instance after your first visit and application for Poor Law Relief, a visitor from the U.A.B. would call at your home to see and assess your personal and household possessions. If after doing so, in their professional opinion, you owned something which they considered to be a luxury, or surplus to your bare requirements, like two clocks, a best Sunday suit, two pairs of shoes, or too many ornaments, even a gold ring on your finger, they would suggest you raise money on them, by either selling or pawning them. There was no shortage of pawnshops in the 1920s and 30s.

When you were given a voucher there was also a number of conditions that had to be adhered to as you used it. Printed on the voucher was a rule that a shopkeeper was not allowed to supply butter, only margarine, and no tobacco could be bought. Some shopkeepers would oblige, by letting you have a packet of cigarettes, or a half ounce of pipe tobacco, and marking it down as something else to the equivalent value.

There were also one or two unscrupulous ones who would charge you an extra copper or two for this illegal service. They knew you were in no position to complain.

When I arrived at my aunt's house in Waterloo, she was surprised to see me on my own, until I started to tell her all that had happened to me; about our house being vacated, and me being sent to foster parents.

'Auntie Alice' Burns with my brother Dick (16), 1930.

A couple of hours after my arrival, and when I'd finished eating a meal, a policeman called at the house, no doubt in response to a surreptitious telephone call that my aunt had made earlier unknown to me. He informed her that the Salvation Army in Norris Green had reported me as missing, and now I was to be taken to a children's refuge in Wavertree as soon as a car was available to take me there.

It arrived within half an hour, and the tears started to flow from me like a leaky pair of lock gates. My aunt kissed me goodbye as I was put in the car then it sped off to Wavertree.

The Children's Refuge was called Olive Mount where I spent the night locked in a dormitory with a score of other children after being given a bath and some washed second-hand clothes.

The following morning after breakfast I was taken for a 15 minute drive to a building very familiar to me, it was Bootle Town Hall, the seat of all power for the district. I was hustled into an upstairs room where a lot of well-to-do people of both sexes were seated around a large table. Because the event was a long time ago, and my mind was in a state of turmoil at the time, the proceedings have become a little vague over the years. I do remember a gentleman wearing a butterfly collar and sporting cat-like whiskers seated at the top of the table. He seemed in charge of the gathering.

He spoke kindly to me and said I would be returning to Olive Mount to stay for a while longer, until a decision could be reached what and where my future was to be. I spent a further two weeks in the Wavertree Home, during which on one occasion only, my newly married sister Jane came to see me. She told me she was now living in two rented rooms over a cake shop in Litherland, and hadn't got the space for me to stay with her. Even if she had, as she explained to me, I had now been placed under the jurisdiction of the courts, and it was they who were going to decide where I was to live. I couldn't understand how they possessed such power, but on hearing this from my own sister I was devastated. When she made preparations to leave I had to be physically held back by one of the nurses to stop me from attempting to follow her. She had been my last hope, and the one person who I thought would not let me down, now that hope had gone.

On the 20th of June 1934, in the Children's Department at Bootle Town Hall, I was *sentenced with kindness* to spend the following three and a half years, in what the man in the butterfly collar described as a lovely Home and School where, he said, I would be educated, taught a trade, and live in until I was 14 years of age.

When I heard the time factor a sense of panic came over me; it was like being given a life term in prison. Even until that moment I'd always thought that before such a thing was allowed to happen someone else in the family, like big brother Henry, would come to my rescue and take me in. I never thought it would end with me being taken away from Bootle altogether to some faraway place, and be put among total strangers. I felt I would die of a broken heart, or be beaten to death for not conforming.

Although I was told I'd meet and make friends with lots of boys my own age, that didn't console me. I knew I wouldn't be going home every afternoon at four o'clock. I felt I wanted to run out of that room all the way home, until I realized for the first time in my short life, I had no home to run to anymore. A feeling of overwhelming loneliness and isolation filled my whole being and I knew at that moment that I had only myself to rely upon. I knew that wherever I was taken I would never stay voluntarily. In a place where there was no Litherland Road, no Bootle Village, or familiar friendly faces I knew so well the place which had all my memories, both happy and sad.

Chapter Four

Introduction to my new home

When the hearing came to an end I was taken to an adjoining room; on the door was a plaque which read: Mr A. Taylor, Child Welfare Officer. By now it was near to 12 noon. While I was eating sandwiches and drinking tea a man and a woman came into the room and started to talk to Mr Taylor, I soon gathered from their conversation that these two people were going to take me to my *school prison*.

When I'd finished eating I was asked if I wanted to go to the lavatory before being escorted to the car, to commence the journey to foreign parts where I was to be left.

In the car the woman sat alongside me in the rear seat while the man, after making sure all the car doors were securely locked, got into the driving seat. The car moved off and soon we were travelling along un-familiar roads.

The lady sitting beside me gave me a bag of sweets but, as I was chewing them, tears were going into my mouth at the same time.

As the miles slipped by she started to tell me about the Home I was being taken to. I guessed from her knowledge of the establishment she had made this journey before, probably with other wards of court.

I was being taken to Barnes Home School, Heaton Mersey, Manchester. That was the postal address then, although Heaton Mersey is much nearer to Stockport, which was in Lancashire, today it is in Cheshire.

All the time my escort was talking to me I wondered if I would ever see Bootle or my family again. The car had travelled what seemed to me to be a long way when it slowed down and turned into a private

Barnes Home School, 1946–nine years before it's demolition.

driveway. As it drew closer to the buildings I looked up and saw the clock tower of Barnes Home School for the first time.

The car pulled up at the Gothic archway oak door directly beneath the clock. On each side of it there were ornamental iron lamp standards. We got out of the car and the woman pulled on the Victorian type bell. The door was opened by a youngish looking female dressed in the black and white uniform of a housemaid.

Barnes Home School was opened on the 2nd of August 1871 by the then Bishop of Manchester. The buildings themselves were designed by Alfred Waterhouse, who also designed Manchester Town Hall. The Home was named after Robert Barnes, a wealthy Lancashire cotton mill owner, who provided the money for it to be built, and was the Mayor of Manchester from 1851 to 1853.

He died at Fallowfield on Christmas Day 1872 aged 72, soon after Barnes Home was opened. He left a fortune of £160,000 to his only daughter.

The Home was built for 'The education and training of destitute and neglected boys.'

The housemaid led us along a hallway and lightly knocked on one of the doors. A voice from inside bade us to 'Come In' and we entered the study of the headmaster of the Home, James Henry Rowe Esq.

He rose from behind his desk to greet both of my escorts with an out-stretched arm and bid them to sit down. I remained standing.

Mr Rowe wasn't a very tall man, he was thick set and had very bushy eye-brows, was about in his mid-fifties, and had an affliction in his left eye, which closed at frequent intervals. As I got to know him better over the following years, I really never knew whether he had an eye ailment or it was just a habit he had when he was scrutinizing and weighing people up.

When the formalities were over with the documents from Bootle Town Hall being handed to the headmaster, the maid was recalled to show my escort out. There were more handshakes, and a 'Goodbye Robert' to me from them as they left the study.

I heard the noise of the car engine as it was started up then it being driven away, leaving me alone with Mr J. H. Rowe. He talked to me for half an hour after the car had left to return to Bootle. He never asked me about myself or my family background. I suppose all he wanted to know would be in the papers he'd been given. The headmaster concentrated on telling me things about the routine and privileges of the school. There was no mention as yet of any administration of punishments.

He expressed the hope that I would settle in quickly, and be happy and attentive during my four year stay. His mention of the time span made me wince with misery. I wanted to correct him, to point out I would be 14 in three and a half years time and not four years, but even that period was too hurtful to mention so I didn't bother.

I was eventually handed over to a much younger man a Mr Foulds, he was one of the 'live in' school teachers, and I was later to learn he was the housemaster of Atherton House the house to which I'd been as-signed .

There were four houses named after governors or benefactors of the Home. Being in Atherton House meant I would wear a blue and black striped tie. The other three houses were Hodgekinson, a red and black tie; Miller, yellow and black, and Byron, green and black.

Mr Foulds was a very tall thin man who wore spectacles and had thick wavy hair, he spoke in a very quiet manner and was a gentle man.

The school lessons were over for the day and he had been instructed to take me to the various departmentsfor kitting out with new clothes.

I was taken first to the matron's surgery, the matron was the headmaster's wife, Mrs Rowe, but the lady who attended to me was the assistant matron, Miss Hollingsworth. She was a tall, heavily built, big bosomed woman, dressed in a light blue and white stiffly starched nurses uniform. Her sleeves were always rolled up, as though ready for any emergency, and she had a lovely pink complexion. She asked my name, entering it in a large ledger, passing a remark as she did so, that the surname of Houghton was a 'Good old Lancashire name.'

I was given a brief body examination by Miss Hollingsworth and, as she was a stranger to me, I found this embarrassing. She said I would be seeing the doctor on his next visit, and that she was to be addressed as Miss Marion. In contrast, the matron herself, Mrs Rowe, was to be called 'Madam'.

From the surgery I was taken to the tailors shop, to be fitted with two different shades of short trousered suiting, and a blue gabardine raincoat. One of the suits was for everyday use, the other for Sundays only. We then went to the linen room for underclothing, shirts, ties, socks, etc. Finally to the cobblers shop for two pairs of shoes, a pair of gym slippers, shoe brushes, and my own tin of shoe polish.

We were not dressed in any uniformity as such, but all boys wore a dark blue schoolboys cap with the distinctive initials B.H.S. intertwined in gold thread on the front.

As the days, weeks and months went by I noticed Mrs Rowe wore a different outfit every day and walked about the Home as if she was the lady of the manor, which I suppose she was. She never appeared to have much time for the boys, except to scold them, and was always very aloof.

The Rowe's had a son and a daughter, in their teens, and the family lived in their own private apartments in the main part of the Home; A part of the buildings where no boy dare venture.

There were 180 boys in the Home, their ages ranging from 7 to 13, and each had a number, I was given number two.

One of the things I remember was that, number one belonged to a boy named Pearson, a Manchester lad. Everything of his: Best suit, Towel peg, Locker, were always next to mine. Pearson was very talented, he went outside to a grammar school for his lessons, he was the Captain of Atherton House, and was two years older than myself. In 1936 he was 14 and left the Home, I've often wondered what he made of his life.

When all of my kit had been gathered I was shown where it was to be kept, then after a few reassuring words from Mr Foulds, I was handed over to one of the boys. His name was Copeland and he came from Waterloo, Liverpool, so we had one thing at least in common.

And so I joined in with the routine of the school, to start what was in my opinion, my sentence.

The main frontage of Barnes Home was on Didsbury Road. It stood back from the roadway, with gardens and lawns in front of the main entrance. The buildings formed a square behind the front, making a large enclosed yard at the rear.

The buildings consisted of dormitories, classrooms, gymnasium, cobblers shop, linen rooms, band room, toilets, etc. Directly behind the clock tower was the large dining hall and the kitchens.

Daily routines and schedules

The weekdays at the Home started at 7am with the duty master switching on the dormitory lights and shouting 'Rise and Shine', then pulling down the bedclothes of those beds where there was no response.

As soon as we had folded our pyjamas and made our beds in the prescribed manner, the routine was to make our way downstairs to the communal washroom for a wash stripped to the waist.

In the washroom were 4 long lines of water pipes which stood about 4 feet from the floor, with a tap approximately every two feet, and a trough underneath to catch the water. We stood at these with a master in attendance. Talking wasn't allowed during ablutions because of the time factor, the washroom could only hold about half the total number of boys at one time. At 7.45 a handbell was rung, by then it was expected that every boy would be ready for breakfast parade, washed, tie in place, shoes polished, teeth brushed, and hair combed. We always paraded in house groups, and in four lines of 11 each house.

The dining hall accommodated all 180 boys at one sitting, and we sat at tables according to which house we belonged. There were 12 boys to most tables, and four tables to each house, making sixteen tables in all, excluding the serving tables.

We sat in age groups. On the first table of each house, sat the first monitor. He looked after the most junior boys; slightly older ones sat on the second table, with the second monitor in charge; then came the third table and the fourth. The last named was also known as the 'top table', and the fourth monitor was the most senior, and Captain of the house.

The monitors were chosen by the headmaster himself, and they moved up a table as they got older, and would eventually become Captains as others left the Home on attaining the age of 14.

When they left, some went into private foster homes, some to work on farms, while others went into the army as boy soldiers, or to Naval land based establishments. One such place that comes to mind, which will become obvious later, is The Wellesley Nautical School, Blyth, Northumberland.

On the breakfast parade, there was a quick inspection by the duty master as we filed into the dining hall, to observe that each individual was neat and tidy. On many occasions, if the master himself had the *morning blues*, he would detail one of the Captains to carry out the inspection .

When every boy had arrived at his respective table we all stood silent behind our own particular chair, and bowed our heads as the master said Grace. 'For what we are about to receive' etc. The order would then be given for us to sit. We sat with arms folded until the order was given for us to 'Carry On', only then were we allowed to talk amongst ourselves as we ate.

On the walls of the dining hall hung large gold gilt framed oil paintings. The pictures were of men connected with the Home, also prominent local figures and business men, one of the paintings was of Robert Barnes himself.

Most of the boys, except the older ones on the senior tables of each house, had the same amount of food to eat, the seniors, however, had larger portions.

On each half of the tables was a plate of bread for six boys, and on each plate there were 18 slices of bread, three slices for each boy. It was a serious offence if a boy took more than he was entitled to. One of the first things we all did therefore, before starting to eat, was to count the number of slices on the plate just to make certain the kitchen staff hadn't mis-counted, which happened occasionally, causing false accusations.

The main meal of the day was served at noon. The boys passed in front of the serving staff who were standing behind trestled tables at the kitchen end of the dining hall armed with large spoons and ladles for the gravy and custard.

At times 'extras', in the form of bread end crusts, would be brought out of the kitchen on a square wooden tray which was placed on a serving table. Hoping to qualify for a crust, a whole table after everyone on it had finished eating what they had to eat, would sit up straight with arms folded, almost like dogs begging, hoping to catch the master's eye. If successful, the master would nod his head to the monitor, as an indication to him to lead all the boys on his table, each one carrying his plate, up to the extras tray, and take a buttered crust from it. When the tray was emptied a muffled groan would ensue around the dining hall. Like all growing boys, we were always hungry.

Breakfast finished at 8.30 precisely, when we stood once more to say a thank you prayer before filing out of the dining hall.

We spent the next half hour in the yard, during which time we would visit the toilets, before going into our respective classrooms at 9am for daily lessons.

For a boy to put his hand up in the classroom before 9.30, with a request to visit the lavatory meant his name going into the master's notebook for future reference. It was looked upon with annoyance that he hadn't availed himself of the opportunity after leaving the dining hall.

We went into classes according to our ages regardless of which house we belonged.

Our main meal of the day, as previously described, was between noon and 1 o'clock, (we did nearly everything to a strict timetable) resuming classes at 1.30.

School lessons finished at 4pm and tea parade was at 4.30, with another hand inspection as we entered the hall.

Leisure activities

After tea in the summer months we spent our leisure time playing in the yard following our own pursuits, perhaps roller skating on a pair borrowed from a boy lucky enough to have them sent in to him by a still caring relative.

We took turns on them, showing off our individual skills. We played all kinds of games or just lolled around in groups reading comics and frequently we talked about ourselves and the different towns and cities we came from, often between sighs of nostalgia and homesickness.

At 8pm it was time for wash parade, followed by a stand-up supper which consisted of a cup of powdered milk and a rock hard biscuit, our name for the biscuits was *dog food*.

On the stroke of 9pm we went up to the dormitories. these were four separate large ward like rooms, divided by fire doors. Here again each house had its own room or dormitory, and all the beds were numbered, numbers 1 to 45 were Atherton, 46 to 90 Byron, 91 to 135 Miller and 136 to 180 Hodgekinson.

In bed we talked or read until lights out at 9.45pm.

In the winter evenings we had the choice of pursuing hobbies and pastimes under cover such as woodwork, basket making, painting, first aid, or learning to read and write music, and to play a brass instrument. This brings to mind the achievement of one of the boys from the Home; he later became the bandmaster of an army regiment.

There were quite a few 'old boys' who came to visit after leaving the home, I was never to be one of them.

During my enforced stay my only ambition was to leave the establishment forever. My favourite hobby was studying road maps and more especially the roads that led from Heaton Mersey to the County Borough of Bootle. In all the three and a half years I spent in captivity I never got over being homesick. This was the main reason why I was to become, (according to the headmaster) the most prolific absconder in the history of the Home.

Sunday was one of the days I liked better than the others because of the change of scenery. At 9.30am on the dot attired in our Sunday best suits we paraded and set off marching behind the band to church. We proceeded along Didsbury Road in rows of four abreast and in house order to St John's Church, Heaton Mersey, and always with lots of the local people looking on.

As we marched, a bag of sweets or a bar of chocolate was sometimes thrust into our hands by a sympathetic member of the public. Although this practice was generally frowned upon by the head and masters alike it wasn't officially objected to. The recipients were later expected to share their good fortune with other members of the same house when we returned but not before.

The headmaster, his wife, and their two children, always went on ahead of the parade in their car, they occupied the same front pew in the church every week on the opposite side to where the boys sat.

Barnes Home boys filled the whole of the left hand side of the church, three or more of the masters sat at the rear, taking note of any misbehaviour, like talking, being inattentive or reading something other than the Bible, perhaps the Comic Cuts or something similar during the service.

One of the ways of enforcing discipline and to encourage good behaviour was a points system used in the Home.

At the beginning of each week commencing on Monday mornings every boy was allotted six points, one for each weekday. Each point was worth a penny pocket money paid out on the Saturday parade at 1pm. The boys still accredited with six points on Saturdays, were allowed out on afternoon leave, from 1pm until 6pm, and were given sixpence pocket money to spend.

Outside visits

On Saturday mornings all the boys eagerly awaited the arrival of the points board displayed in the dining hall window every week at 10am. On the board in alphabetical order were the names of every boy in the Home. Alongside each name was the number of points accredited for that week. It also showed the previous weeks totals and was an annual and permanent record of the points awarded and lost in a year. Its function helped to give a general assessment of a boy's behaviour.

During the week if any boy committed a small misdemeanour, he would be penalized by being booked by one of the masters, which meant he would lose a point and a penny pocket money. For the loss of two points in any one week, he forfeited two pence plus his Saturday afternoon leave. Most boys preferred a slap on the face as an alternative (which we sometimes received instead). You might be booked for some triviality one day during the week, then the master concerned would relent and show compassion by not reporting the fact to the compiler of the points board, a Miss Whiteman the office secretary, especially if it happend to be that particular master's weekend off duty and he was feeling in a compassionate state of mind.

Miss Whiteman also displayed the *Letters and Parcels* notice in her office window to notify us that these items had arrived for those fortunate enough to have relatives or friends to send them.

We were only allowed to go within a three mile limit from the Home and most boys went to the local picture house to see the special Saturday afternoon children's matinee. The price of admission was two pence.

There was one small cinema in Wellington Road, Heaton Norris, and two more in Mersey Square, Stockport we had the choice of. We were not permitted to go into Manchester five miles to the north.

On a few occasions this rule was broken and boys were observed in Manchester City Centre by someone connected with the Home, perhaps one of the masters. They would be ordered to return to Heaton Mersey at once and then reported to the headmaster.

For such an infringement which was regarded as a serious breach of the rules the minimum punishment was the loss of 12 points which meant two weeks pocket money forfeited and four weeks loss of Saturday afternoon leave. For a repeated contravention, the punishment was much more severe, and three strokes of the birch across the backside in addition.

The number system was mainly for the re-distribution of clean clothing. All our wearing apparel, boot brushes and even the individual tin of shoe polish, was either ink marked or stamped; all of mine with the figure 2. Each boy had his own open-fronted locker in the locker room. This room also served as an under cover parade hall in place of the yard, when the weather was inclement. In the numbered lockers we kept our second pair of shoes, running pumps, gym shorts, two shoe brushes, and the tin of black polish. These items had to be laid out in a certain way at all times so as to give an instant sighting for inspection purposes. Mr Wright, our own cobbler, was the person who carried out the inspection.

He was a non-academic well into his fifties and always walked very quickly with short steps. I imagined he was capable of being a tap dancer, at least he knew all about shoes! He wore gold rimmed spectacles which he looked over rather than through, and always wore, in a different shade of white, a very stiff Victorian collar.

He went round all the lockers once a week with his notebook and pencil looking at the state of repair of all the shoes, jotting down the number of the locker where shoes were in need of attention at the same time observing that all the kit was complete in each locker. If any article was missing, the boy concerned was called upon to give an explanation and to find the missing item or items forthwith. It would probably be found in another boy's locker, put there as a boyish prank. When Mr Wright's pencil was not in use it was kept behind his ear.

Some time later, his assistant Mr Alsop would follow collecting the shoes and taking them to the cobblers shop. Mr Alsop was very rarely seen without his leather apron except when I saw him going home at 5pm, I remember thinking at the time I wish I too was going home.

Exploring backgrounds

Quite a number of the boys were orphaned, one had been found abandoned as a baby, parents unknown. But most boys like myself came from broken homes in town and cities all over England and Wales.

In any gathering of boys of ages up to fourteen years there will always be a small percentage among them of 'wet the beds'. These boys are afflicted with an uncontrollable physical weakness, caused by a weak bladder or emotional disturbance. It results in the inability to be awakened in the night for the need to urinate, and as a consequence this occurs in bed without them being conscious of doing it. There are still people around who wrongly assume that boys who wet their beds do so because they're too lazy to get up and use the toilet. This kind of thinking was more prevalent fifty years ago, today we are somewhat more enlightened. Boys with this weakness usually grow out of the embarrassing habit by the time they reach fourteen as their bladder grows stronger. I've been told it effects boys rather than girls.

Out of the total of 180 boys in Barnes Home School in 1934 there were about six or seven wet the beds and I was unfortunately one of them.

Of all the rules and regulations made for the boys to observe in the Home, most of them were necesary and fair, excepting in my opinion one. This was the rule where a boy was penalized and punished by losing a point and a penny pocket money every time he wet his bed. It also meant if he did it just twice in any one week, he lost the privilege of Saturday afternoon leave.

Besides this penalty we had to suffer the indignities, taunts, and name calling by both staff and boys alike. Crudely we were called 'piss the beds'. A further embarrassment was experienced when we took our wet bed sheets to our own laundry and were pilloried by the female staff, who were workers brought in from outside. They looked upon us as causing them extra work so we weren't received very favourably when handing in the wet sheets. Myself, and the other boys so afflicted, were given a *Kidney and Bladder* pill to swallow every morning but they did nothing to cure the weakness. I was almost fourteen before I out-grew the humiliating ailment.

It was the humiliation and more specifically, the penalties imposed, together with the homesickness that were the root cause of my never being able to settle down in Barnes Home.

It was in 1937 when I'd been in the Home for two and a half years, and had by then absconded sixteen times, the headmaster informed me I had now become the most prolific absconder in the history of the Home.

In contrast that same year I was given a copy of Charles Dickens' *A Christmas Carol*, by my classroom teacher Mr Partridge for being the best behaved boy in the class! That is, when I was present in the class-room and not on the run.

Chapter Five

My first 'Break'

One of the questions new boys were asked by the others was: 'what part of the country do you come from?' You tend to strike up a special relationship and bond with those lads who hail from the same town as yourself. I quickly learned from a couple of *Bootle Bucks* and *Liverpool Scousers*, that it was almost forty miles from Heaton Mersey to the Liver Buildings at the Liverpool Pier Head and the Dock Road where I used to collect horse manure. To a ten year old forty miles sounded an awful long way especially as I knew I would have to walk it to see Bootle again. An intention I had, even before I arrived at Heaton Mersey. I had two strong legs, determination, and I wasn't daunted by the realism of having to do it.

I planned my first break out after studying a road map of Great Britain in the classroom.

It was seeing the close proximity of the town of Wigan to Heaton Mersey that decided me to make for there as soon as I was out and on the road. My reasoning was that when I was in my family home Wigan had been frequently mentioned in conversation, it was the place my father travelled to on his barge from Liverpool. I knew that once I reached the canal towpath at Wigan, all I had to do was tread its route in the direction of Liverpool and it would eventually take me to Bootle without any fear of getting lost. There was also the possibility that somewhere along the canal I might meet up with my dad and ask him to do something to release me from *my bondage*.

Besides studying the geography of the land outside the Home I had also paid close attention to the location of the doors and windows inside and the types of locks and catches on them and also where they led out to.

On the fourth night after my arrival—June 24th, 1934—I absconded for the first time.

It was about 1am in the morning when everyone was sleeping I got up from my bed and went as if to go to the lavatories at the end of the dormitory. Instead, carry my clothes and shoes, I negotiated the stairs that led down into the yard. The dormitory doors were never locked at night in case of fire. I dressed in the yard toilets then made my way to a classroom window which I had unlocked during the day. The window was situated in the play yard, across the other side of the classroom was another window, this led out on to the garden path which circled the gardens. The gardens themselves were cultivated with potatoes and other vegetables to help feed the boys and staff. After lifting up the window in the yard I climbed through letting myself into the classroom pulling the window down behind me. There was a clock on the wall which indicated it was 1.30am, far too early for a ten year old to be seen on the streets so I sat at one of the desks having a *sit up snooze* with one eye open watching the minutes tick away.

At 5.30 it was daylight and I could hear the noise and movement made by the horse and carts as they made their way to Stockport Market with farm produce on the cobblestones outside.

I thought it was now time for me to be on my way before the whole of the Home was awake. Climbing through the second window, I jumped down on to the garden path. I can't recall whether I pulled this window down behind me or not. I do remember running across the gardens as fast as my legs would carry me. I imagined as I ran that a hundred pair of eyes were watching me from the windows of the large private houses that surrounded Barnes Home. Once I'd reached Wellington Road and was a couple of miles away on Stockport Road leading to Manchester I breathed a little easier and felt safer from detection and capture.

Leaving my prison without having had breakfast I well remember the lovely mouth watering and appetising smell that came from the McVitie and Price biscuit factory on Stockport Road as I passed by.

That same factory of fifty years ago is still in operation and giving off the same beautiful aromas of fresh early morning baking.

By the time I reached the centre of Manchester walking through Piccadilly and Deansgate throngs of people were making their way to work. Consulting my pencilled notes on a scrap of paper and looking at road signs I made my way across the River Irwell into the City of

A milestone at Wigan–one of the 125 positioned along the canal.

Salford. The tramcars were rattling along in the middle of the roads displaying to me what were strange sounding names on their destination boards: Names like Irlam O'th Heights, Pendleton, and Walkden.

Approaching Atherton I saw trolly buses for the first time. They had long poles running on electrified overhead wires just like the Liverpool tramcars but, instead of running on tram tracks, they had the new type of *pumped up* tyres and wheels on them. In contrast to the rattling tram they were very quiet as they moved along, so much so, I thought they were very dangerous because you couldn't hear them approaching.

It was the middle of the afternoon when I came to the outskirts of Wigan. One of the first things I noticed was that the majority of the people, men, women, and children, were wearing clogs, with each individual making his or her own clatter on the pavements.

I came to the brow of a bridge on top of which was a public house called *The Seven Stars Hotel*. At first sight I thought it was a railway bridge but as I got closer and peered down a walkway at the side of the bridge I saw a path running alongside. I had stumbled on to the Leeds and Liverpool Canal which would lead me all the way to Bootle.

Displayed on the towpath only yards from the bridge was a triangular metal sign, it denoted that in one direction Leeds was 91 miles from that spot, and in the other direction Liverpool was 37 miles. I knew of a simi-

H & R Ainscough's iron boat 'Viktoria' at Appley Lock, 1960. Lock Keeper's house on right; Mrs Bowen's cottages obscured by horse.

lar sign which read Liverpool 3 miles; this was on the gas works wall at Bootle. The numerals on each side of these milestones added together always totalled 127¼.

By now I had been walking for nine hours and had no idea how many miles I'd covered. I was very tired and hungry, but being on the canal side had given me renewed energy and spirit because I felt safer from detection than on the public highway. It was if I was 'far from the maddening crowd'.

As I left Wigan behind me and headed for the open country, I met and passed barges being pulled by horses; sometimes only one of the two man crew would be visible steering the boat with the other out of sight down below in the cabin. After scrutinizing the person at the helm as I passed, I would ask if *Dick Ranty* was known to them and if they had any idea of his present whereabouts? Only one bargee suggested he was in Liverpool discharging a cargo of coal. At least I felt I was getting nearer to him all the time.

It was difficult to recognize some of the bargees under the comical headgear they wore, women included, (who were equal to men in performing the work) dressed in their ankle-length skirts, petticoats, and frilly bonnets tied under the chin so as not to have them blown off by the wind.

I'd been walking for about an hour since leaving Wigan and was now pasing cultivated fields. I entered a field and helped myself to a turnip and, rubbing the soil from it, I stopped and sat and ate it sitting on the gates of Dean Lock at Gathurst. I thought just then what a lovely spot it was. There were no noises of civilization only the mating calls of birds and the trickle of water as it leaked down the lock gates. It was years later when I first saw the painting of John Constable's *The Haywain*, I was reminded of Dean Lock.

After consuming the turnip I lay behind a hedge and fell asleep. When I awoke it was getting late in the evening but as it was mid-summer it didn't go dark until after 10pm. The light was just beginning to fade as I resumed walking feeling better after my rest, and with a tummy full of fresh turnip but I was very thirsty. I was almost tempted to sample the canal water but thought better and decided to wait until I came to a house or cottage. It was now quite dark and there was a moon shining on the water. As I approached what I now know to be the village of Appley Bridge, lights were twinkling on the opposite side of the canal and I could make out the outline of a factory from which came a very unpleasant smell. The local people called it the *bone hole*. It was a factory where the bones of animals were rendered down to make glue. The smell, combined with a warm summer's night, made the aroma more obnoxious.

Although I was very thirsty I couldn't find enough courage to knock on one of the cottage doors to request a drink of water. I imagined in my young mind I might knock on the door of a policeman and that wouldn't do me any good. I've often thought since that it was fate that made me pass by those cottages at Appley Bridge and continue on for another two hundred yards when I came to Appley Lock Cottages.

As I walked the path that runs alongside the elevated lock there was a row of six small cottages. A 3ft high wall stood in front of the cottages separating them from the towpath. Beyond them in the direction of Liverpool there was only inky darkness.

A most eventful meeting

It had started to rain and my thirst was getting worse, I was also very wet. In desperation I knocked on the door of number two where I'd seen a dim light in the window. The door was opened by an old lady who wore ankle-length clothes and a shawl covering her shoulders. She peered out at what had become a dirty night. From the glow of an

Mrs Bridge – mother of some fine boatmen.

ornamental paraffin lamp inside the cottage she was able to make out my small frame standing at her door. I said to her: 'Could I have a drink of water please?' Ignoring my request she said: 'Where have you come from lad?' Speaking in a very tired voice and with a very wet body I replied quite simply: 'From Manchester Mrs.' With a surprised look on her face she then asked in a broad West Lancashire accent: 'Are thee by thee sen lad?' and in my Liverpool jargon I answered: 'Yes'. Then she said: 'Tha'ad better cum in lad thart wet thruf'.

As I stepped into the tiny dim-lit room of the cottage I was invited to sit in a chair by the side of the welcoming coal fire. The old woman said to her husband: 'He's walked from Manchester', with that she went out of sight and into the back kitchen, saying as she went: 'I'll put 'kettle on'.

The old man sat weighing me up for a few seconds then said: 'Hasta walked it ort way then lad?' and I replied: 'Yes' noticing at the same time he was dressed in the garb of a canal boatman i.e. a heavy dark blue seaman's gansy and khaki coloured corduroy trousers. A pair of brass buckled clogs were at the side of his rocking chair as he sat in his stocking feet with an unlit pipe in his mouth.

He asked which part of Manchester had I walked from. When I replied: 'Heaton Mersey', he said he'd never heard of it. I mentioned Stockport to him; then he said: 'Why, that's t'other side o' Manchester fro' 'ere. Tha'as had a good hike lad'. I nodded in agreement.

The old chap quizzed me on which places I'd walked through, as if checking my route, to confirm I had indeed walked all the way.

Somehow I felt comfortable seeing the type of people they were which led me to believe they were the same kind of country stock as my mother and grandmother, and I had no hesitation in telling them the truth of how I had run away from the Home.

Before I commenced telling of the events leading up to and why I'd been taken to Heaton Mersey the old ex-bargee said to me: 'You're not from Manchester are thee?' When I said I was from Bootle, he said: 'I thowt so, I con tell th'way thar spakes'.

There was a clatter of plates coming from the back kitchen and the old lady emerged laden with sandwiches and cake. I was asked to take off my wet coat which was promptly put over a chair by the fire to dry out. Addressing her husband she told him: 'Let the lad eat before he talks he must be clammed'. At that I tucked into the corned beef sandwiches, the cake and the lovely hot mug of tea.

When I'd satisfied my hunger and thirst I started to tell Mrs Ann Bowen and her husband Tom how I'd been taken to the Home only days previously and how I had *escaped* in the early hours of the morning.

Eventually when I told them of my family being boat people and that my dad was still working on the canal their interest grew. Mrs Bowen asked: 'What did you say your dad's name was?' and I repeated: 'Dick Houghton'. Ann Bowen looked at her husband and said: 'Isn't that Dick Ranty's real name?' and before Tom could answer her I said: 'Yes, that's right, that's what he's called'. Mrs Bowen slapped her knees with both hands and let out an exclamation of: 'Well I'll be' then said to me: 'Your mother's name was Ann same as mine wasn't it?' To which I replied: 'Yes I think so but she's dead now'. Mrs Bowen gave me a sympathetic look and said: 'I know she is lad. You wouldn't remember her would you?' I replied: 'No'. She turned to Tom and said: 'This must be one of Ann's lads, he must be the youngest'.

I thought I was knocking on the door of total strangers to ask for a cup of water and they turned out to be one time old friends of my mother in days long past.

Tom and Ann Bowen had spent all their working life on the canal, retiring when they were in their sixties and were now in their seventies. As was the custom they too had acquired a nick-name. They were known the length and breadth of the *cut* as Tom and Ann 'Shiney'. It was because of their visible fanaticism in keeping everything on the boat spic and span and shining. All the fixtures and fitting i.e. the stove inside

Tom Bowen ('Old Shiney') with his horse behind Appley Lock Cottages. c. 1929.

the cabin, pots and pans, the decks and walkways on the boat, and especially the ornamental brasswork both in the cabin and on the horses tack.

Mrs Bowen went on to tell me that for a short period during the 1914-18 war when the canal was frozen over, she and my mother worked together in Bootle Gasworks employed in shovelling coke because thousands of men from the area had been called up to fight the war in France. Speaking more of my mother Mrs Bowen said she'd had a hard life, the cause being mainly my father's hard drinking habits.

Because of the proximity of the cottages to the canal and the lock the Bowens had a good view of the traffic that negotiated up and down it, Up for Leeds, Down for Liverpool. It was a factor not missed by one of the barge owning companies. They installed a telephone in the cottage and employed the elderly couple as agents and observers. This Liverpool based company, and others who shared the cost, would contact the cottage to enquire if a certain barge had passed through the lock and perhaps its approximate time. Or to pass on a message to a certain boat captain to instruct him, for instance, which colliery to head for to load a particular grade of coal, or which warehouse to proceed to for other

Canal Transport Warehouse, Wigan Basin—now the "Wigan Pier" Pub.

types of cargo. Barge captains were instructed to call at the cottage to use the telephone and call their office for orders.

And although the Bowens were officially retired they still had an interest in the goings on of the canal for which they received a small remuneration. The Bowens asked me a lot of questions and midnight came and went. Because of their knowledge of the movements of the canal traffic they knew a *Wigan Fly* boat was due down the lock at about 2am en route for Liverpool.

These boats were so named because they were diesel engine driven and sailed to a strict timetable. This particular *Fly* left the Canal Transport Warehouse at Wigan Pier at midnight every weekday with cargoes to be delivered in Bootle or Liverpool the following morning. It sailed through the night non-stop reaching Bootle at 8 or 9am the time depending, and subject to a possible few factors, like the tonnage carried, the wind, the performance of the engine, and the fan (propellor) not being fouled by some of the rubbish in the canal, and the time consuming operation cleaning it while the boat was stopped.

The inception of this method of carrying cargoes was an attempt to compete with the ever growing competition from the railways.

Tom and Ann Bowen decided that when the sound of the engine of motor boat *Irwell* was heard as it approached Appley Lock they would hail the captain or his mate who they knew to be brothers Harry and Tom Baybutt. The intention was to explain to them who I was then to solicit their help by requesting them to give me a lift to Bootle.

As predicted, just before 2am, the silence was broken by the throb of a motor boat's engine. Eventually Canal Transport's boat *Irwell* entered the lock. Appley Lock is the last lock on the descent to Liverpool. It is also the deepest.

The powerful headlight perched on the bow deck pierced the darkness of the night as the gates were closed behind *Irwell*, locking her in. A conversation took place between the Bowens and the Baybutts on the brough of the lock. I was introduced to the Baybutts as *Dick Ranty's lad*. When the iron boat had lowered to the Liverpool level the gates were pushed open and she sailed out to be brought to the canal side allowing me to step aboard.

Mrs Bowen gave me a shilling as I said 'Goodbye' to them both and promising I'd let them know how things went for me either by letter or other means. Tom Baybutt led me down into the boat's bow cabin where I was shown the bunk bed where I was to sleep the night away. We sailed on through the darkness passing through Parbold, Burscough Town, then alongside the Aintree Racecourse and finally on to Bootle with the beam of the bow headlight showing the way around the twists and turns.

Despite the throbbing of the engine at the stern end and the vibration it caused I soon fell into a deep sleep.

Hours later I was awakened by the wonderful smell of cooking. I sat up and peered out of the bunk to see Harry Baybutt siting in front of the tiny cabin stove holding a frying pan over it. When he saw me he said: 'Now little mate didta 'ave a good slumber?' I assured him I had.

Harry continued: 'I thowt the smell would wak thee up. You'd best get up and have some breakfast we'll be in Bootle in another hour or so and we wont put thee off on dry land with an ompty bally.'

The captain, brother Tom, was up top on the tiller steering the boat. It would be his turn to eat when Harry relieved him.

When the *scoff* was ready Harry told me to get *stuck in* to the bacon, eggs and home-made bread washed down with a large mug of tea whitened with tinned condensed milk. While we were eating on the pull-down table harry told me that both he and his brother had known my late mother and her family. They too had been born and reared in Burscough Town. They also knew my father. Harry passed the remark: 'Your father's a rum bugger", no doubt referring to his drinking. Harry

Iron boat 'Everton' passing through electrically operated Lift Bridge, Litherland, 1944.

quickly finished his meal and donned his funny hat in preparation to taking over the tiller.

The hat worn by the majority of the bargees was a trilby without a dent in it. The brim was pulled down back and front, which shielded their eyes from the wind and stopped the rain going down the back of their neck as they stood on the stern deck manning the tiller at the mercy of the elements. Ex-army greatcoats were the most favoured garb worn by boatmen, these were bought extra long perhaps only inches from the ground to keep their legs warm. A bargees dress would be similar to the American Hill-Billies.

Eventually we both left the *forrid* cabin and walked the fourteen inch wide gunwhale *(gunnel)* to the stern end. I sat on the engine house top basking in the early morning sunshine.

As the boat moved along at the leisurely speed of approximately three miles an hour on that late June morning, Harry informed me that under the tent shaped black tarpaulin sheeting *Irwell* was carrying crated machinery bound for Australia, via the Liverpool Docks.

There were more buildings on both sides of the canal after we'd passed under Gorsey Lane Bridge at Sefton, with the inevitable public house on its brow. This one was officially *The Tailors Arms* but it was better known as *Cooksons* by its frequenters because the landlord, the son of the previous one, was named Jimmy Cookson.

Like the bargees themselves, nearly every stone bridge, wooden swing bridge, and single lock had unofficial names. Names like *Old Bob's Bridge, Old Dustys, Sam's Lock* and *Adam's Lock*, titles that were steeped in the two hundred year old history of the canal.

We had just passed through and under the newly completed electrically operated steel lift bridge at Litherland and were now passing the dozens of uninhabited coal barges tied alongside the gasworks wall on the towpath side. These boats were laden with different types of coal from small slack to large lump coal. All of it destined for the furnaces of Bootle Gasworks, to manufacture gas and the by-product coke.

All these boats belonged to John Parke & Sons and had been towed the two miles from Bankhall where they were loaded with coal from railway wagons, which had in turn been loaded at the Lancashire and Yorkshire coalfields.

Boats were also loaded at the Bankhall sidings for other local destinations such as Liverpool Gasworks at Athol Street, The Distillers Company in Vauxhall Road, and for Tate & Lyle's, who owned their own boats, some of them the largest on the canal, with a carrying capacity of over 80 tons.

As we neared Litherland Road Bridge at Bootle which was to be my disembarkation point, Tom and Harry Baybutt wished me well as I prepared to leave. I assured them I would be all right and that I intended to make my way to my Aunt Alice's house in Waterloo. They reminded me to keep in touch with Tom and Ann Bowen who would keep them informed.

I jumped off the *Irwell* as she went under the narrow part of the bridge and thanked them for the ride and their hospitality as they continued on in to Liverpool.

Moments later as I walked along Litherland Road I came abreast of the window that had once been my grannie's parlour and the family home now empty and vacant. It made me feel very melancholy.

I got on to the Stanley Road bus route and bought a penny scholars ticket to Waterloo.

A visit to my auntie

My aunt who answered the door in response to my knock was, to say the least very surprised to see me.

Litherland Swing Bridge, 1900. This preceded the electrically operated Lift Bridge
and is now a modern flyover.

As I sat in the house I told her about my being sent to Heaton Mersey and how I'd made my way back to Bootle. It transpired she already knew of the misfortunes that had befallen the family and she attributed it all to my father.

I pleaded with her to let me stay at her house and go to school from there. Like sister Jane she explained how it was impossible. Unknown to me then, Aunty had a son and a daughter, she had put them in the Blue Coat School, also in Wavertree, and close to Olive Mount Children's Home. Years later when I was able to understand, besides being a nurse and a widow she was a *career woman* and hadn't got much time for children, not even her own. So there was no chance of me being taken in by her.

I had been sitting in the house for a couple of hours and just finished a meal when there was a knock on the door. Aunty opened it and was followed back into the living room by a tall well-dressed gentleman. As he entered he remarked: 'He has arrived then' meaning me. Within a few minutes amidst a torrent of tears I was led out of the house and into a waiting car. I was taken to the local police station in Church Road, Waterloo. It was there I had my first of many experiences of being put in a cell. On this occasion however the thick solid door was left ajar.

As I sat in the white tiled cell I could hear people talking at the end of the corridor in the station itself. I supposed they were all policemen until I heard the familiar voice of my aunt and the rattle of keys then the sound of the gate at the end of the passage being opened before my aunt was brought to the cell and left alone with me.

She was resplendent in her nurses uniform and had brought me a bottle of *Vimto* and some sandwiches. She sat down beside me on the wooden bench and informed me I was being kept at the station to await an escort to take me back to the Home.

There was the ever present tears as I ate the sandwiches and drank the pop. After a while aunt said she would have to leave because she was due on duty in Liverpool's Stanley Hospital and it entailed a half hour bus ride to get there. She kissed me goodbye then was gone leaving me alone in the cell once more.

Early that same afternoon Mr Arden, one of the masters at Barnes Home, arrived accompanied by a lady. She was his fianceé and had come along just for the ride. With the formalities completed I was put into the car and we started off for Heaton Mersey. In a little over an hour we drove up the driveway of Barnes House.

I remember thinking to myself; After all this time and effort it had taken me to arrive at Waterloo now in a fraction of the time I was back where I started from. Of course the route taken by my escort did not include Wigan and we travelled a lot faster than did Fly boat *Irwell*.

I was take right away to the headmaster's study where the first object I sighted as I entered was a 3ft long cane standing in a corner behind his desk at which he was seated. I was ordered to stand directly in front of him. Firstly he wanted to know how I got out of the Home, at what time did I leave and by what means did I arrive at Waterloo? He also wanted to know if I'd committed any acts of dishonesty while I was away?

To the question of my mode of travel; I told him I'd walked all the way and the route taken was the same as the car that brought me back. I told this deliberate lie with the future in mind and not wanting to implicate Tom and Ann Bowen and the Baybutts or the canal waterway route.

Thinking ahead I thought the next time I absconded a car might be dispatched in an attempt to catch up with me before I got too far. If that happened and the car took the Altrincham Road which was due west, I would be walking north to Manchester and Wigan Pier.

Introduction to punishment

When Mr Rowe had finished interrogating me the time had now arrived for him to announce punishment. He commenced by proclaiming that the penalty for absconding was six strokes of the birch on the backside but, he added, in view of the fact I was a new boy, and had not yet had time to adjust to being in the *School*, as he always called it, and because I was not yet eleven years old, he was going to show leniency by ordering that I receive only two strokes to serve as a warning.

In full view of the boys who had had their tea and were playing in the yard I was taken to the gymnasium by Mr Rowe and Mr Arden, the latter carrying the birch. The object of making a spectacle of me I thought was to deter any other would-be absconders.

Once inside the gymnasium I was ordered to take off my outdoor trousers and don a thinner pair of gym knickers. The headmaster ordered me to bend forward and touch my toes then instructed Mr Arden to commence the punishment.

When the first stroke landed on my posterior I jumped up like a scalded cat. It felt as if I'd been stung by a hundred wasps. It took me a few seconds to compose myself before complying with the order to again bend over to receive the second stroke. The punishment over, I changed back into my ordinary trousers with great difficulty and discomfort.

Mr Arden was instructed to take me to the surgery where I was to suffer the further indignity of having to drop my trousers this time for Miss Hollingsworth to examine my backside to see if there was any broken skin or bleeding. I observed in a mirror later that my backside had two black and blue stripes across it.

For days afterwards when I sat I had to lower myself very slowly and very gently.

After the surgery I was taken back to the headmaster's study where my name was entered in the punishment book then signed and counter signed by Mr Rowe and Mr Arden.

Before being let loose to join the other boys in the yard I was warned by the headmaster that I could expect more strokes if I went A.W.O.L. again.

Almost immediately I was surrounded by some of the other *inmates* who wanted to know all about my exploits and the punishment. Each boy had his own particular question to ask for instance; How far did I get, How did I arrive there; What was the birch like and will I ever do it again? One boy, John Copeland, who like myself was Bootle born wanted to know if I went on the run again could he go with me?

In all my later *break-outs* I always went alone.

Life-saving letters

Every morning and afternoon excepting Sundays when the *Letters and Parcels* list was displayed in the office window which faced out into the yard. If it had not been for Mrs Bowen, over the following three years, I would have scanned it in vain because she was the only person who bothered to write to me. In her fortnightly letter she always enclosed a shilling postal order to be put into my school bank account to enable me to buy sweets from the tuck shop and for a penny postage stamp to answer her letter. The headed notepaper and envelopes we used were supplied free. In special circumstances at the headmaster's discretion the stamp also.

The fact that Mrs Bowen could read and write a little was an achievement, because most retired boat people could not.

All our letters and parcels were opened and read by the headmaster before being given to us and all monies and postal orders taken out and credited to our account.

At Christmas time those with relatives or approved friends were allowed to spend two weeks leave with them, returning after the New Year. Free travel warrants were provided by the Home's governing body. Each boy going on leave was given a document stating the leave was authorized as we were all wards of the courts.

Special treats were laid on for the 40% of the boys whose circumstances meant spending Christmas within the confines of the Home. There was of course the Christmas dinner in a decorated dining hall, with crackers to pull, paper hats to wear and a warning to be careful of the silver threepenny pieces in the Christmas pudding. Silent cinematograph films were shown on a portable screen erected in the dining hall.

On certain afternoons we walked two abreast along the pavement to Mersey Square, Stockport to see a matinee showing in the picture house. During my first Christmas at the Home in 1934 I saw my first Tarzan film starring Johnny Weismuller and Maureen O'Sullivan entitled *Tarzan and the Apes*. Another day we went by special buses to a Manchester theatre to see the pantomime *Puss in Boots*.

Every year in July all the boys and most of the staff spent two weeks under canvas in North Wales. We travelled by special train from Stockport to Penmaenmawr where thirty or more round white tents, each with paliasses and blankets were erected in advance of our arrival, always in the same field within sight of Puffin Island.

Litherland Road, 1905.

The tents were arranged Indian fashion in a circle with two marquees in the centre, one larger than the other, the smaller one served as the kitchen and the other as the dining hall.

Every day during the two weeks, parties of about thirty boys with a master in charge would start out in the morning with a packed lunch in haversacks and go on rambles to different beauty spots. One party would climb Mount Snowdon another to see Swallow Falls or to visit the castles of Conway or Caernarvon. We also went on trips to Rhyl and Bangor and to the slate quarries of Llanfairfechan and many more places. During the holiday every boy would visit each of these places.

The daily routine of the camp began at 7.30 when we were awakened by a bugle call. We washed in cold water in bowls filled from specially erected standby taps. After dressing we rolled our paliasses and folded the blankets before going to the marquee for breakfast. At 8.45 we had kit inspection, each boy's kit was rolled up identical and set up in rows outside (weather permitting). Each boy stood behind his own kit as it was inspected by the headmaster. Prizes of slabs of toffee were given every day to the tent who, in Mr Rowe's judgement, had the neatest kit.

Over the period of two weeks everyone received a slab of this toffee. For me the irony of the toffee was that it was manufactured and packed by Williams Toffee Ltd situated in Waterworks Street in Bootle Village. The factory itself was situated only a hundred yards from what had been my family home. The smell from the works used to penetrate into our living room.

After eight months in the Home I had my eleventh birthday. It was February and the daylight hours were lengthening and I was very homesick for Tom and Ann Bowen and the streets of Bootle again. Mrs Bowen was still writing to me every second week trying to console me by saying that time would soon pass but, to me, it seemed to do the opposite. My thoughts (which were never too far away from it) turned to absconding for the second time.

I was not the only boy to run away from the Barnes Home but none did it so often as I did, and the older I got, the more I seemed compelled to do the bunk.

Understandably we talked a lot amongst ourselves especially in the yard when there was less chance of being overheard by the masters. I heard stories from others who originated from places a lot further away from Heaton Mersey than Bootle and had run away. Places such as Newcastle-upon-Tyne in the north east and one as far south as Cornwall.

When they were on the run in their endeavour to reach their home towns they jumped on passenger trains at either Stockport or Manchester after purchasing a penny platform ticket. These tickets were obtained from vending machines situated in most major railway stations. They enabled the purchaser to go through the ticket barrier and onto the platform alongside the trains themselves. They were used by scores of young enthusiastic train spotters who hung around major stations in the days of steam hoping to get a glimpse of the mighty locomotives and make notes of the name and numbers and sometimes, as an added bonus, to obtain the signature of both the driver and fireman, but especially the driver.

I decided that on my next planned *walk out* I would give the platform ticket idea a try.

I'd saved a few pennies from my weekly pocket money instead of spending them on sweets. I intended to buy food when I was on the road to keep up my strength which I felt was more essential. By now, and after a lot of careful study, I had discovered quite a lot of ways of leaving the Home un-noticed.

Chapter Six

A second try for freedom

It was mid-afternoon on a cold February when I absconded for the second time. I boarded a Corporation bus in Wellington Road, Heaton Norris, bound for Piccadilly Manchester. I knew it would be at the 5pm tea parade before I was missed which gave me a two hour start on any pursuers.

Using a platform ticket it was my intention to board a Southport stopping train at Manchester and get off at Wigan. I arrived at Piccadilly Station only to find that the train I wanted left from London Road Station on the London Midland and Scottish Line (L.M.S.). Asking my way I arrived there minutes before a Southport Stopper was due out. Just enough time to purchase a platform ticket from a machine.

I went through the barrier showing the ticket and walked alongside the locomotive as if admiring it, attempting to act the part of a train spotter. I also had one eye on the ticket inspector at the barrier watching to see if he was showing any interest in my activities but his attentions seemed to be elsewhere.

As preparations were being made for the train to depart the porter walked the length of the train slamming the doors shut, this was the moment for me to hop into one of the 3rd class carriages. Even at my tender age I realised the game would be up if I went into the 1st class compartment because, dressed as I was, I would be noticed at once as not belonging there. As I seated myself in the corner of the non-corridor carriage on my own the guard blew his whistle, the engine driver responded with a toot on the steam whistle, and the train moved slowly out of the station.

I was on my way to Wigan and by a much quicker method this time. After the train got beyond Wigan it would stop at Gathurst then Appley Bridge. Giving the matter some consideration I thought it would be safer to leave the train at Wigan and walk the remaining five miles, because on the small rural stations the ticket collector doubled up as the porter, station gardener, and general worker. They stood on the platforms waiting for the alighting passengers to hand him their tickets or show passes. Most of them were on first name terms with him. Any strangers would be conspicuous to him.

It was better to be safe from capture than sorry so I got off the train when it stopped at Wigan and went immediately into the gent's lavatory and into one of the cubicles. The cost was another penny. I sat there for about twenty minutes and when things seemed quiet I ventured out onto the platform again (Over the years it was a form of action I took many times).

At Wigan Wallgate Station the only way out was through a barrier situated on top of a flight of stairs which led out onto Wallgate itself. I looked up and saw it was un-manned. Climbing the stairs I walked through the exit and out onto the road. Had I been challenged, I would have produced the platform ticket telling the inspector I'd been train spotting and hoping he wouldn't scrutinize it too closely and see it had been purchased at Manchester.

Once outside the station standing on Wallgate proper I asked one of the clog-clad Wiganers the way to the canal. He gave me a bit of a strange look as he pointed out the direction and muttered 'Down Yonder'.

I started to walk in the direction *the mester* had indicated, and within minutes I arrived at Wigan Pier. I strode off in the direction of Liverpool along the towpath feeling very pleased with myself when I thought of all the miles I hadn't had to *pad-hoof it* on this occasion.

It was about 8pm when I knocked on the door of number two Lock Cottages. Mrs Bowen opened the door and on seeing me she gave out an exclamation of: 'Eh, it's little Bob again. Come on in lad'.

Tom Bowen was sitting in his favourite chair facing the small windows where he could see 'th' boaats gooin up and darn th' lock'. Old Tom greeted me with: 'Hello little mate hasta floon coop agin?'

Mrs Bowen asked him to keep his voice low before explaining to me that her son-in-law, Jack Spencer, who lived next door at number one was a special constable. He was married to Margaret (Maggie), Mrs Bowen's daughter, and they had three schoolboy sons.

Jack Spencer worked at the linoleum works at Appley Bridge and assisted Sergeant Sharpe, part time, at the Bridge Police House. Apparently Jack had been told of my last visit only after I'd been put aboard the motor boat *Irwell*; he had explained to Tom and Ann that because I was a ward of court their kindness amounted to a breach of the law, and by aiding and abetting me to escape it could prove serious for them.

I sat eating another meal provided for me but I was not at all happy at hearing that the law lived next door. I felt as soon as I satisfied my hunger I wanted to be *legging it* along the towpath regardless of the time, the weather, or any other reason.

Old Tom seemed to enjoy my company and my ear as he related some of the happenings which had occurred during the sixty years he spent on the canal with his wife Ann as his mate. The unlit pipe was in his mouth because Ann wouldn't allow him to light up in the confines of the small cottage. She said: 'He fills th'house full of smook' which made her cough. When he wanted to smoke he had either to 'goer onth cut bank' weather permitting or 'inta stable' at the rear of the cottages.

Tom spoke of my dad, when my dad was 'no' but a lad' helping boatmen around Liverpool Gasworks and how he grew up a bit wild with apparently no-one to chastise or guide him.

Tom Bowen was born in 1866 and was sixteen years older than my father.

Since being told of the special constable living next door I now regarded Appley Lock as changed from a safe haven to a danger zone and the thought saddened me.

Apprehended

It was now turned 10pm and dark outside, there had been no mention of putting me aboard another *fly boat* to transport me to Bootle. While I was analysing the situation realizing the old couple wouldn't want me to leave at that hour, and in the dark to walk the canal bank, there was a knock at the door. Instinct told me before the door was opened by Mrs Bowen that it was bad news for me and so it turned out to be because in walked Police Sergeant Sharpe from Appley Bridge accompanied by special constable Jack Spencer.

They found room to sit down and started to talk to Tom and Ann while, strangely, I was ignored. Towards the end of the chatter the sergeant suddenly turned to me and asked: 'Why have you run away from the Home, don't you like it there?'

Tom Baybutt (3rd from left) — Captain of iron Fly Boat 'Irwell'
sitting with his pals on the Don.

I thought the question didn't warrant an answer so he never got one.
When the law decided it was time to leave Mrs Bowen turned to me and
said it was for the best pointing out the perils and dangers that could
befall me on the road or the canal towpath at night.

Before the sergeant, Jack Spencer and myself left to walk the path to
the Police House Mrs Bowen said she was going to write to headmaster
Rowe to ask if it was possible for me to leave the Home and offered to
take me in and send me to school in Appley Bridge along with her own
three grandchildren. She assured me she was also coming to visit me at
Heaton Mersey and have a talk to Mr Rowe.

Putting another shilling in my hand she wished me good luck as I left
between two policemen. I could also see she too was upset.

When we arrived at the police house I was lodged in the sergeant's
living quarters with his wife and six foot tall son Robert.

While the sergeant made a telephone call Mrs Sharpe started to talk
in a friendly manner to me. In the meantime Jack Spencer said
'Goodbye' to me and took his leave back to Lock Cottages.

An hour later nearing midnight a car arrived to take me to Police
Headquarters at Wigan. On arrival I was ordered to turn out my
pockets. The total contents was a shilling piece and a platform ticket.
The desk sergeant at Wigan looked at the ticket and guessed im-

mediately why I had it in my possession, I just confirmed his suspicions admitting the free train ride from Manchester. He put questions to me that became standard, whether I'd perpetrated any dastardly deeds during my brief bid for freedom, such as travelling on the railway without a valid ticket, after which I was eventually locked in a cell for the remainder of the night.

The following morning was Sunday and it was about mid-day when headmaster Rowe himself arrived accompanied by Mr Eckersley another of the masters. They must have missed morning church service to make the journey, that fact wouldn't have pleased Mr Rowe.

The journey from Wigan to Heaton Mersey passed quickly travelling via Bolton and Manchester. The boys had already lunched when we arrived, I was given a late dinner on a table in the kitchen.

The captain of Atherton House, George Pearson, was sent for and given instructions not to let me out of his sight until bedtime at 9pm. It wasn't a job he relished because it curtailed his own activities and leisure time until then.

That night I was locked in a small room in which was a single bed, a chair and a chamber pot.

On the Monday morning at 9am when the boys went to their respective classrooms I was instructed to stand outside the headmaster's study. I stood for what seemed an eternity before Mr Rowe entered, and still longer before he ordered me in to stand before him as he sat behind his desk. I was surprised he was alone I fully expected a *punishment administrator*, in the guise of one of the masters, to be present also.

Partial Reprieve

When he started to speak he first drew attention to the time wasted and the expense incurred by the Home etc., etc., before he informed me of a telephone call he'd received from Mrs Bowen. He said during the conversation with her she had implored him not to birch me and he had reluctantly promised her not to do so. Mr Rowe gave his reason for bowing to her request, it was because she was an elderly lady, and she had told him about her friendship with my late mother and her sad life before her premature and untimely death.

He went on to say that for a trial period and during my leisure time I was to be given certain jobs and chores to carry out. It was hoped the measure would serve more than one purpose, one it would enable a better surveillance to be kept on my movements and two keep me better occupied instead of trying to abscond. It would also contribute to offset some of the expense in having to retrieve me from scattered police stations.

Mrs Bowen had asked the head about the possibility of my being fostered out of the Home into her care. Such a request he had told her would have to be put in writing and submitted to the board of governors for their deliberation at one of their quarterly meetings; and only a juvenile court was authorized to give a final decision.

A feeling of great relief came over me when I was dismissed and told to report to my classroom for lessons without first being thrashed with six strokes of the birch.

I now began to nurture the feeling that I had something to look forward to with the possibility of being released and going to live at Appley Lock Cottages. A few days later I had a letter from Mrs Bowen saying, weather permitting, she would be coming to see me in two weeks time on a Saturday.

To get from the cottages to Heaton Mersey required a mile walk from the lock to the road bridge along the towpath; then it was an uphill climb to Appley Bridge Railway Station to catch the stopping train to Manchester, a slow laborious journey. From Manchester it was a half-hour bus ride alighting on Wellington Road, Heaton Norris and finally a fifteen-minute walk to Barnes Home.

For Mrs Bowen it must have been a very tiring journey taking a supreme effort but her fortitude and energy were typical of most boat women.

It wasn't possible for her husband Tom to accompany her, at 70 he had arthritis in one leg and walked with the aid of a stick, as he was heavily built he found walking an effort.

There were express trains direct from Southport to Manchester, stopping only at Wigan Wallgate, these were nicknamed *Daddies' Trains* by the locals. The name was given to them by the domestics working in the houses of business men who lived in Southport and worked in Manchester. The children named the trains and the domestics followed suit.

On Mrs Bowen's first visit she arrived at noon. At the time I was roller skating around the yard on a pair lent to me by my pal Louis Gladwin who came from Halifax in Yorkshire.

One reason we became pals was because we had both arrived at the Home on the same day and were both put in Atherton House. We were both 10 years old and our beds were next to each other in the dormitory, we spoke a lot to each other about our family backgrounds.

Tom Draper (second from left) and other Burscough Boatmen.

I was summoned to the headmaster's study, this time for a pleasant reason. When I entered Mrs Bowen was already seated talking to the head. To my great joy he informed me I was to be allowed out for a few hours in the company of Mrs Bowen for a walk into Stockport. I was cautioned not to let anyone down and be back by 5pm as she had a train to catch at 6.30 from Manchester. I was instructed to go and spruce myself up and be back in ten minutes.

We went to Mersey Square and to a small shop for tea and buns and had what was for me a most wonderful time. We arrived back in plenty of time for her to catch her train. She saw Mr Rowe again before she left and thanked him for his kindness before starting back on a journey I wished I had been making with her.

The assistant matron Miss Marion (Hollingsworth) had an assistant nurse Miss Clare and they both shared a small sitting-cum-dining room. As decreed I was given a number of chores to perform before and after classrooom lessons. My first allotted task after I'd had my breakfast, was to go to their sitting room and clean out the fire grate, removing the ashes and resetting it with newspaper, wood and coal ready for lighting. I had to carry out these tasks before going to my classroom to be marked in the register as present by my teacher Mr Partridge for lessons at 9am.

Soon after I commenced this seven mornings a week duty I began to receive praise from both Miss Marion and Miss Clare, later I was given small gifts like a bag of sweets or bar of chocolate. Miss Clare started to buy me a weekly boys' book called *The Wizard*. At that time there were a number of similar weekly books specially published for schoolboys. *The Adventure, The Hotspur, Comic Cuts* and the *Film Fun*, the latter depicting the antics of Charlie Chaplin.

When school lessons finished at 4pm, every weekday and at the weekends I was given other jobs in the kitchen and the dining hall. In the kitchen I helped prepare the vegetables for the following day, for this I was often rewarded by being given extra food by the cook-in-charge Mrs Nye, this were always welcome.

One of my favourite occupations was to go around the sixteen dining hall tables with the 180 places armed with a seven pound stone jar of jam. The job was to cleanly deposit a measured blob of jam on each plate with a large spoon, as demonstrated to me by the cook who said there was sufficient in the jar to serve all 180 plates.

At my first attempt as I got near to emptying the jar a feeling of misery came over me because as I scraped the jar clean there was still a whole table with empty plates. Hurriedly I had to retrace my steps taking a fraction of jam from each plate to make up the deficit. When I'd finished the plates looked a sorry mess. After more practice, I was skilled enough to distribute the 180 portions with micro-like precision and lick the spoon at the conclusion of the operation.

Week-end Break

It was because of carrying out the domestic jobs in her sitting room Miss Marion started to take an interest in my family background. She enquired from me one day if I received letters from home or if I ever had any visitors? When I mentioned Mrs Bowen and where she lived she became more interested.

It transpired that she had a married sister living in Standish with whom she spent some of her off-duty weekends and the village of Standish is only a couple of miles from Appley Bridge.

One Friday morning just as I'd finished cleaning out her fire grate she came into the room and told me it was her weekend off commencing the next day. To my surprise she asked me if I would like to spend Saturday and most of Sunday with Mrs Bowen, adding she had obtained permission from the headmaster to take me with her. I could hardly believe my ears, I began to think this might be a prelude to my leaving the Home for good and living permanently at Appley Lock.

By 9am the following morning I was ready, attired in my Sunday best suit, sitting in Miss Marion's room awaiting the car that was to take us. On schedule it stopped outside the main entrance, Miss Marion's brother- in-law was driving the small Ford car accompanied by his wife.

We set off in the direction of Manchester sitting comfortably in a car that had been affectionately nicknamed the *Tin Lizzy*. When we arrived at Appley Bridge the car was driven along the towpath to the lock. Fortunately we did not meet any horse drawn boats because if we had it would have meant reversing back to a wider part of the path by the bridge allowing the horse, which had priority, to proceed.

I spent a very happy and enjoyable weekend with Tom and Ann Bowen getting to know their three grandchildren, Horace, Eric and Cecil, and being acquainted with the neighbours who lived in the other four cottages.

In 1937 the weekly rent for each cottage was one shilling and sixpence (7p). All six were owned by Tom and Ann Bowen. Like most canal- side cottages there was no piped water, gas, or electricity in them.

During my weekend stay I made myself useful by chopping *kindling wood* for starting the fire and carrying drinking water in two white enamel buckets kept especially for that purpose. The water had to be carried from a fresh water spring which ran alongside the canal 100 yards along the towpath from the cottages.

Access to the spring was made by descending six stone steps leading from the canal towpath. Most boatmen knew of its location, and often stopped their boats, both horse drawn and diesel powered, to fill their fresh water casks.

The buckets I carried for the Bowens helped fill the multi-coloured wooden cask that had once adorned the stern cabin deck of their horse-drawn boat. It was kept next to the horses' provender box, both painted in the same gypsy caravan style and colour. The name *Ann* was painted on them in Gothic lettering to denote the name of the boat to which they belonged. Now they were part of the cottage's back kitchen furniture. Tom Bowen was an *owner carrier* and his boat was named after his wife.

Sunday on the canal was like any other day of the week. Boat people worked on that day because all their employment was done on a *piece work* basis. They had no hourly, daily or weekly rates of pay, they were paid by the amount of tonnage and the distance it was carried.

The simple rules of employment were, No work. No pay.

They saved their days off for when any one of them, including the horse, wasn't feeling well, there was no such thing as Sickness or Holiday pay.

It was interesting to watch the boats go up and down in the lock and the way in which the two man crew worked in unison, each one knowing by practice exactly what to do, and the order in which to do it, in order to safely negotiate the locks. It could be easy for man or boat to have an accident if the operations were not carried out properly.

In the 1930s, approximately 50% of boat crews were a combination of man and wife or father and son or all three.

As arranged, Miss Marion and company arrived on the Sunday afternoon to take me back to Heaton Mersey. Her sister and her brother-in-law came into the cottage for a short chat with Tom and Ann before we left. For the first time I went back to the Home with a light heart and with happy anticipation for the future. These thoughts, however, were to be short lived.

Disappointment and dashed hopes

It was three weeks later when I went to spend my second weekend at the lock. Mrs Bowen said she had received a letter from headmaster Rowe, it stated he had been informed by the governors that they, after going into all the circumstances, considered the Bowens were too advanced in years to be foster parents to a 13 year old boy. The letter was short and sweet.

The decision was devastating to me. Tom and Ann Bowen and daughter Maggie tried to comfort me but I'd already made up my mind on the course of action I was going to take.

My compelling urge to be free was far greater than any other consideration, greater than any punishment that could be meted out to me.

The last thing I wanted to do was to hurt or upset the Bowens or Miss Marion Hollingsworth but by the time the latter called to collect me on this occasion I was miles further along the canal bank trekking my way in the direction of Liverpool.

As I walked, I just hoped people would understand my obsessive reason for leaving the way I did after all their kindness to me.

It was a warm summer evening as I passed the Packet House pub on Burscough Bridge, the hotel was so named because of the steam packet

Burscough Bridge; 'Packet House' pub on left (now 'The Admiral Lord Nelson').

boats that used to ply the canal before the diesel engined boats. Cargoes of grain were transported in them from Liverpool Docks to Ainscough's flour mills at Burscough and Parbold.

The next cluster of houses after Burscough was New Lane a mile further on. It is a small community, having its own pub The Farmers Arms, wooden swing bridge, and a shop at the end of a row of cottages by the side of the canal. It had its own railway station (New Lane) on the Southport to Wigan line where trains stop every two hours. The long row of cottages were inhabited mostly by bargees.

I continued on until I came to Scarisbrick Wood one side of which runs alongside the towpath a short distance from Ormskirk. By now it was late evening going dusk and I was ready for some sleep. I spent that night in the wood with my back propped up against one of the hundreds of trees dozing the night away. For company I had the birds, badgers, bats, rats, rabbits, owls, squirrels, field mice and foxes, so I did not feel alone.

Whenever I passed the wood many times years later as a bargee myself, I could always pick out that particular tree against which I rested as a thirteen year old fugitive.

The daylight came early in the morning and I roused myself from my slumber and emerged out of the wood and onto the canal bank.

I set off scrutinizing the produce of the fields looking for my favourite *eating out* breakfast of either turnip or carrot.

Walking long distances in the peace and quiet of the countryside gives you the time and inspiration to think. My thought were on where my sister Jane was living now she was married, the best person I thought would know would be my Aunt Alice. I decided to pay her another visit solely for that reason, minding not to stay too long because of her habit of telephoning Waterloo Police Station letting them know of my whereabouts.

As I walked in the early morning daylight, it was still only about 6am, I encountered a number of engine powered boats making a good start to the day, perhaps having to reach a destination in a Lancashire or Yorkshire mill town in time to visit the local music hall. Some of the boats' crews were unattached and had a girl in more than one mill town. I was looked at with curiosity by the men at the tillers. Seeing one so young and up so early was not something they saw very often.

I was far too young and too well dressed in my short trousered suit to be mistaken for one of the many tramps that walked the length of the waterway especially in the proximity of Ormskirk Workhouse.

Sad to relate I never did reach my aunt's house that day. As I was approaching the built-up area of Litherland, (next to Bootle) I was suddenly confronted by two men who seemed to come from nowhere. It was obvious they had been tipped off, probably by one of the suspicious early morning boatmen, I don't really know.

I arrived in Bootle all right, not as I anticipated, but with a police escort.

I was promptly placed in the cells in Bootle Town Hall the place where my incarceration began almost three years previously.

for the first time part of my escort back to Heaton Mersey was Mr Wright of the cobblers shop. He'd taken his pencil from behind his ear for the trip but was still wearing his stiff Victorian collar.

Before I received my six strokes of the birch for this latest escapade the headmaster told me how I'd let everyone down, especially Miss Hollingsworth, who had arrived at Appley Lock only to find, *I'd floon coop agin*, to use Tom Bowen's vernacular.

The person who carried out the punishment on this fifth occasion was a Mr Parkes who was the woodwork teacher and also played rugby football for the Heaton Moor club. The boys knew him especially for his frequent spasms of bad temper and the heavy handed slaps he gave us. He had all the attributes of a fourteen stone bully and although he sat with the rest of the masters in their common room he was a non-academic.

I lost favour with Miss Marion and Miss Clare and also lost the job of cleaning her firegrate with all the little perks that went with it. The weekly boys' book bought for me by Miss Clare was stopped also. In today's terminology it would be said: *I was in the dog house*. I was made to spend more time helping in the kitchen but I got to like working there.

I remember Mrs Nye the cook-in-charge who always seemed grateful for the help I gave. I think she felt sorry for me, it was well known that I'd had the birch more times than any other boy.

Mrs Nye was a woman who never got flurried or flustered and I never saw her lose her temper. At odd times, when perhaps I was working the potato machine she would come alongside me and place a titbit of food for me to eat.

Even at our tender ages amongst the boys there were one or two *barrack room lawyers*. It was one of these, Tom Morgan from Cwmbran in Wales, who enlightened me to the fact that under the rules of punishment no boy could be birched more than once in a period of three months. And the maximum number of strokes to be administered at any one time was six.

Tom was still in the Home when I left it. I've often wondered what he made of his life. Perhaps he enlarged his talents and became a Q.C. or even a judge.

Altogether I received the birch seven times in Barnes Home, the first time two strokes then, six strokes six times.

The punishment never for one moment deterred my urge to run for freedom, and, as I got older the birch became easier to endure.

I will never forget how I once boarded a train at Manchester in possession of a penny platform ticket. As the train pulled into the station the destination boards on the side of the carriages included the name Liverpool. I was all tensed up at the time in fear of being observed boarding without a valid ticket. I wanted to leave Manchester as quickly as possible in case the police had been alerted to be on the look out for me. I got on the train in a state of half panic just before it departed and stood in the corridor, always alert, watching and listening for the ticket inspector and his dreaded shout of *All Tickets Please* as he made his way along the carriages.

I always positioned myself standing in the corridor in the middle of the carriage so that whichever direction the inspector came from it gave me time and the opportunity to take evasive action like locking myself in the toilet or hiding under one of the seats in an empty compartment, if I was lucky enough to find one.

On this occasion I stood looking through the carriage windows watching the countryside flash by. An hour later I thought it was time I was seeing the familiar landmarks of the outskirts of Liverpool, instead I was looking on to green fields. I began to get a sickening feeling and realised that I was on the wrong train. My fears were confirmed when the train pulled into Crewe station, the train I was on was bound for London not Liverpool. It came into the station on an end platform with a brick wall on one side. A porter was shouting *All Change Please*.

It was said in the 1930s: 'Wherever you travel by train in Britain you have to change at Crewe'. Of course it wasn't strictly correct, but Crewe was a very large terminous.

I had no alternative but to leave the train along with the other passengers and could see that there was only one way to go and that was in the direction everyone else was heading, towards the only exit and ticket barrier at the end of the platform.

All tickets had to be shown before continuing to London on another train and from another platform.

As I followed the passengers to the exit I felt like a cornered fox. I couldn't turn and walk in the opposite direction nor could I stand still, my only option was to try bluffing my way out through the barrier by telling the inspector I'd lost my ticket.

As I approached him in an endeavour to persuade him how sincere and genuine I was, I started to dig in all my pockets in search of a non-existent ticket. The fact that I was a short trousered twelve year old travelling alone on a London bound train did nothing to support my image.

When I told the inspector of my supposed loss he asked me to stand on one side, inside the barrier, until the remainder of the passengers had passed through.

I continued the palaver of digging in my pockets at the same time looking for the slightest chance to make a run for it.

Because I hadn't produced a ticket by the time everyone else had passed through his barrier the inspector requested me to accompany him to the railway police office.

I started to walk alongside him for a few yards then I made a dash forward. The inspector shouted; 'Stop that lad'. Another uniformed railwayman, he could have been the current Olympic sprint champion by his show of speed because he made me look slow in comparison, caught hold of me and between them I was frogmarched to the police office.

After being questioned as to my name and destination and how much did I pay for the lost ticket, etc., I realized pretence was futile. I told the railway police the truth, especially when they found the platform ticket in my pocket.

I was eventually taken to what had become my second home, the local nick, although of course Crewe was a new location to me.

After more questioning at Crewe Police Station I was locked in a cell for the night where I had plenty of time to reproach myself for jumping on the wrong train.

Chapter Seven

Apprehension and arrest

The following morning I was informed, to my surprise, I was to appear before the local magistrates in the juvenile court to be charged with defrauding the London Midland & Scottish Railway of their rightful fare.

At the subsequent court hearing the bench were told I was already a ward of the courts and an absconder from Barnes Home.

The magistrates, when given all the facts, remanded me to the police cells to await an escort back to Heaton Mersey and the Home.

A coincidence of this escapade was that the ticket inspector who apprehended me and who gave evidence in court had the same christian and surname as my own, Robert Houghton.

Mr Rowe and his assistant headmaster Mr Arden came for me in the 1934 Rover car registration number JA 471. I've never forgotten the number. It was the model which had an impression of a wheel pressed into the cover of the boot in which the spare wheel was kept. In the centre of the boot cover was the red triangular crest of the Rover Car Company.

The car spent a good deal of time parked at the main entrance of the Home beneath the clock tower with the two ornamental wrought iron lamp standards with their bulbous glass shades. when the Home was completed in 1871, they were probably originally then lit by gas but converted later to electricity.

For most of the journey back I was ignored as I sat in the back seat of the car. I overheard the headmaster mentioning to Mr Arden the time and expense incurred in the present operation and then giving a quick backward glance in my direction to see if I was listening and to perhaps to install in me a feeling of guilt.

The only feeling I had at that moment was one of self condemnation for jumping on the wrong train.

When we arrived back after my absconding, the stipulated time of three months since I'd been given six strokes on the backside had not expired, in fact it was only six or seven weeks and the soreness from those strokes had barely healed. I was taken to the headmaster's study and without further ado was given two stinging strokes of the birch one on each hand then told to report to Mrs Nye in the kitchen to be put to work.

This was the winter of 1936, the days had become cold and the long dark nights had once more returned.

One day in December of that year all the boys left their classrooms and assembled in the dining hall. There was to be a speech on the wireless at 3pm by the new King Edward VIII, King of Great Britain, Northern Ireland, Emperor of India, and the Dominions Overseas, etc., etc.

He told us he was giving up the job of being King to marry an American woman named Mrs Simpson, his brother George was going to take over in his place. I remember it was the first time I'd heard the word abdication, it sounded to me like the name of an ointment.

Opening Mersey Tunnel

This occasion took my thoughts back to 1934 when, as a schoolboy in Bootle before I became a waif, the children of Hawthorne Road Council School were taken by tramcar to Liverpool to see his father King George V and Queen Mary open the Mersey Tunnel. Each boy was given a paper Union Flag on a stick to wave.

Christmas arrived and a lot of the boys went on home leave for two weeks. I often wondered why those who went home were ever sent to Barnes Home in the first place, but that subject, and the reasons, were never spoken about in the Home. As always I was one that had to remain, in fact all my privileges had long since been taken away even my penny a day pocket money had been stopped. I always had a few pennies in the bank which had been sent to me by Mrs Bowen and I was allowed to have threepence a week on a Saturday to buy sweets.

The master whose turn it was to open the tuck shop was given my pennies to make sure they were spent on tuck and not saved for platform tickets or bus fares to Manchester. In addition, Mrs Bowen had been sent a letter telling her that it would not be advisable for her to visit me until further notice.

She never failed to write to me in her spidery handwriting most weeks, which I very much looked forward to.

It was now the Spring of 1937, a time of year that always brought on my homesickness stronger than ever. I would long for the days when I was at home in Bootle and how after I came home from school at 4pm and had my tea, we kids would play together in the street until called in by our parents one by one for supper and bed.

I used to remember all the things I did in the light nights and I wondered if my old pals ever thought of me and felt so sad I wasn't amongst them anymore. Such thoughts and memories gave me a pain in my stomach.

I had my thirteenth birthday in the February, The two and a half years I had spent in the Home seemed like a life time, even the ten months I had to go to my release, seemed an eternity. I hadn't seen Mrs Bowen for six months but the thought of absconding, and making my way to Appley Lock was ruled out because of the special constable living next door to her.

Since being apprehended at Crewe Station I had been put off jumping on trains without paying. The thought had crossed my mind that appearing in courts too often charged with fraud could result in my being sent to a far worse place than Barnes Home, maybe a Borstal Institution, and I certainly didn't want that.

I never wanted to defraud anyone, all I wanted was a normal home to go to every night with relatives and friends.

Further plans

The geography of Britain had long since been one of my favourite subjects and I especially knew the county of Lancashire. On my next already planned *walk out* I decided on a more direct route to Bootle. Foresaking the Leeds and Liverpool Canal I intended to take the public highway via Cheadle, Altrincham, Lymm, Warrington, Rainhill, and Prescot. Once there to cut through onto less major roads bordering the estates of Lord Derby at Knowsley and that of Lord Sefton at Croxteth. Then it was only 4 miles to the County Borough of Bootle.

The first time I walked this route I realized how much nearer Bootle was to Heaton Mersey using the roads. For each mile on the roads you have to cover two miles on the canal, although I did feel safer on the waterway where the people hunting me never seemed to look for me.

During my *lay up* in the winter months I'd given some thought to the Prescotts, who were cousins living in Pine Grove, Bootle Village along-side the toffee works.

I hadn't seen my elder brothers Richard and George for almost three years and the eldest of the family, Henry, I had not seen for a much longer period, I could hardly remember what he looked like, nor did I know the whereabouts of my sister Jane since she married.

The houses in Pine Grove were even smaller than those on Litherland Road. They were like little boxes with their front doors opening directly onto the pavement. It was as though someone had tried, and succeeded, in building as many houses in the smallest possible space.

They were built on one side of the Grove only; the full length of the opposite side was taken up by Williams Toffee Works. At the bottom was the Bootle Corporation Refuse Depot, better known as the muck yard. When you entered Pine Grove you encountered two contrasting smells, one was the smell of confectionary, the other was of rotten fruit and sewage.

Some of the many Cheethams aboard 'Plato' at Burscough Bridge, 1910.

My Aunt Catherine Prescott, (née Cheetham) was one of my mother's sisters. She too had died in her early forties and, like my mother, left behind a young family, three boys and two girls, the eldest was Doris.

Like my sister Jane, when her mother died Doris was left to act as mother and housekeeper to the rest of the family, Ivy, Henry, William, and John, whilst their father, my Uncle Harry, went to work.

Uncle Harry was a bargee, but his boating did not entail any distance travelling. He was employed by John Parke & Sons barge owners. They were contracted to carry coal in their horse drawn boats from Bankhall sidings to Liverpool and Bootle Gasworks just a couple of miles away. Harry Prescott went to work every morning returning in the evenings.

When I eventually arrived at Pine Grove, not bothering to call on Lord Derby or Lord Sefton as I passed their mansions, I knocked on the door of the Prescott household which was opened by cousin Doris, she was nineteen. At first she didn't recognize me standing there in my well tailored short trousered suit, black leather shoes, grey socks, collar and tie. To the locals I must have looked like Little Lord Fauntleroy.

There wern't many children in Bootle Village dressed as well as I at that time. 1937 was still the days when quite a lot of the kids went around in their bare feet, and the only clothes they had on would be a pair of trousers and a jersey, probably without underclothes. In some cases, even the pants they wore would be a pair of their father's *cut downs*. That was about the size of their wardrobe, as was mine before I went into the Barnes Home.

This is how we were dressed when we used to stand outside Bootle Gasworks, on the corner of Litherland Road and Marsh Lane at 5pm. As the men filed through the narrow doorway, there was always half a dozen of us lads waiting to ask if they had any of their wrapped lunch, left over. Our plea was 'Any Lunches Mr?' In response some of the men would just shake their heads, others would dig in their pockets and hand us an un-eaten *butty*. A lot of times the bread contained brawn, a cheap sandwich filler in those days. As you ate them you could taste as well as smell the gas.

I was made welcome by Doris and the rest of the family as I entered the Prescott's house, Uncle Harry was at work.

I told them I was on leave from the Home. I don't think they believed me but it didn't matter they were still glad to see me. Uncle Harry also welcomed me when he came in from work. He and my dad were drinking partners when my dad was in Liverpool.

I stayed the night at the Prescott's house sleeping three in a bed with Henry and Billy. The following morning, after a breakfast of tea and toast, gladly shared, I suggested to Henry who was a few months older than myself, that we go to Waterloo to see our aunt, where we would be sure of a bite to eat, and maybe get a couple of coppers with which to go and see the Saturday afternoon pictures.

Daniel Parr with Ainscough's boat horse at Burscough.

Henry's mother, my mother and Aunt Alice were sisters. We looked upon her as our posh relation with her living in the better class district of Waterloo, in comparison to Bootle.

We set off to walk the 3 miles to the sea shore; on the sea front north of Waterloo, were Crosby, Hightown and Formby. There were detached houses along the promenade facing the sea, which had verandahs, some with fixed telescopes on them. These were used for looking out to sea to observe the passing merchant ships and the famous passenger liners of the time, bearing familiar household names, going in and out of the Port of Liverpool and Liverpool Bay.

A large number of these *front houses* were occupied by ex sea captains, who enjoyed watching the ships go by. Some of these old sea dogs had travelled the oceans of the world, and had commanded famous ships like the Aquatania, Adriatic, Empress of Britain, Georgic, and Rena Del Pacifico; most had started their seafaring days on sailing ships.

Aunt Alice wasn't a bit surprised to see me, by now she had learned to expect me at any time of the day or night although she did give Henry a puzzled look. She said later she thought Henry was another Barnes Home boy I'd brought with me. Poor Henry wasn't as well attired as myself and she hadn't seen him since the death of his mother, when he was only a small child.

We sat down to tea and cake and Aunty made a very important announcement. She said a *bobby* had called the previous evening to enquire if I'd arrived at her house or had she any knowledge of my present whereabouts because I'd gone missing again. I was now a well-known fugitive at both Waterloo and Bootle Police Stations.

As soon as I heard this I was anxious to be away for fear he might call again while I was there.

Before we left I asked Aunty not to tell the police I'd been there. Her answer was non-committal.

It was 1.30 in the afternoon so Henry and I, after being given a kiss apiece and a shilling to be shared, hurried off in the direction of Bootle in time for the 2 o'clock pictures.

We bought some sweets and paid tuppence each at the *Sun Hall* on Stanley Road. The official name of the picture house was *The Imperial*. Why it was called *Sun Hall* I never did find out.

There was another cinema in Marsh Lane called The Palace which was five minutes walk away. We called it the bug house, the name was self explanatory. The same cinema has since been renovated and today serves as a community centre, while most of the others have either been pulled down or were fire bombed by the Luftwaffe in the 1940s. Some have been turned into Supermarkets and Bingo Halls, and I know of two that have been converted into funeral parlours and Chapels of Rest. A stark contrast to showing films to live audiences.

Henry and I came out of the pictures after seeing Gary Cooper in a film called *The Plainsman*.

With the remaining pennies left over we took home a handful of fish and chips for the Prescott household. Doris buttered some bread, made a pot of tea, and we all tucked in to a popular cheap meal.

Afterwards the Ludo and Snakes and Ladders boards were brought out of the drawer and we all started to play happily until there was the inevitable knock on the front door. Cousin Doris opened it to find two burly *scuffers* (policemen) standing outside. They had been sent from Bootle Town Hall to apprehend me.

(We called them scuffers because we children often got a scuff round the neck from them for committing some small misdemeanour).

I could only guess where they got the information I was at Pine Grove. The shame of it for me was, for the first time in my life, at thirteen, in full view of my cousins and some of their neighbours a pair of handcuffs were put on my wrists.

By midnight that Saturday I was firmly tucked up in a starched white sheeted bed locked on my own in a small room at Barnes Home. I was feeling very lonely after the events of the day and desperately longed to be sleeping three in a bed at the Prescott's house, amid plenty of laughter and family conversation, instead of where I was at that time. All I had to look forward to now was to stand in front of the headmaster and take the punishment he would pronounce.

I should like to make reference to my twenty-first and penultimate time of absconding.

Annual holiday

It was in July 1937 the time of the year when the whole Home left Heaton Mersey for the annual two weeks under canvas in North Wales. We were to embark by special train from Stockport and started marching off four abreast along Didsbury Road to the station, on these occasions without the band. Each boy had a haversack on his shoulder containing a towel, second shoes, polish, brushes, a toothbrush, etc. Clean linen, underclothing and shirts were sent a week later by a hired van and dirty clothes were returned in the same manner.

When we arrived at Penmaenmawr, the sight of 180 boys assembling outside the station to march to the camp, always created a great deal of interest among the local people and the holiday makers.

The thing I remembered most as we approached the camp was the numbered white tents erected in a circle and also the appetizing smell coming from the marquee kitchen; after the train journey we were ravenously hungry. As soon as we deposited our haversacks on top of designated paliasses in allotted tents we queued up in single file, each boy carrying a white enamelled plate and mug, to be filled with what Liverpudlians would describe as a plateful of scouse or Irish Stew.

We took a thick slice of bread from a tray and had the mugs filled with tea from a giant tea-urn. After our first meal we were paraded and given the usual lecture on standards of discipline and behaviour to be observed during the two weeks stay. This was because of happenings in previous years when there had been complaints made to the head-master by local residents, especially farmers, about boys trespassing on their cultivated fields and also chasing cows and sheep.

I always noticed the numerous supply vans displaying Liverpool addresses that travelled the road adjacent to the camp. I knew the position of Penmaenmawr to Liverpool which is linked by a coast road all the way to Birkenhead, via Colwyn Bay, Rhyl, Prestatyn, and Flint, then through the Mersey Tunnel.

This was my third time at camp and I'd been on all the daily rambles that were the routine. I would sooner stand on top of St George's Hall or the Liver Buildings to see if I could make out Snowdon Mountain in the distance than vice-versa, or watch water cascading down Appley Lock on the Leeds and Liverpool canal than to see Swallow Falls or the Fairy Glen.

The thought of being so close to my home town and not being able to visit was an extra antagonism to me.

In the middle of the night before we were due to return to Heaton Mersey I got up and made as if to go to the latrines, carrying my clothes, I made my way out of the camp and along the main highway.

It was mid-summer, and daylight came soon after 3.30am as I walked away from Penmaenmawr, it was an uphill climb for a time, then the road eventually levelled. I reached a point where I looked down and saw some of the night lights of Colwyn Bay twinkling.

Approaching a bus shelter I stopped and sat in one corner out of sight to await a more reasonable hour for walking inconspicuously. As I passed through Old Colwyn, already some people were going for a swim in the sea, shops and cafes were preparing to open for the day. There was a smell of bacon being fried, a taste I would have relished just then, but I hadn't got a penny to my name. I had to make do with eating some discarded orange peel, but when you're really hungry almost anything can taste delicious.

It was a long walk to Birkenhead, especially on an empty stomach, and I didn't see any fields with vegetables to sustain me or they were not as accessible as on the canalside.

By 8am delivery vans, which had started out at an early hour from their depots to deliver bread and cakes to the coastal resorts, were now returning to Liverpool.

I started to thumb a lift. It wasn't long before a Taylor's Bread van driver acknowledged my upraised arm and stopped to pick me up. I remember telling him I'd lost my return ticket to Liverpool and also my money. He could tell by my accent, the same as his, where I came from and that was all that mattered.

We drove through the Mersey Tunnel and this was my first experience of going under the River Mersey rather than on it via the ferry boats.

The driver put me off with a cake in my hand in the centre of Scotland Road by Paddys market amongst the ankle-length skirted, darkly dressed women wearing shawls that abounded in the area in the 1930s.

Tom Lamb from New Lane with his boat horse.
(Note 'swingle tree' (towing bar) at rear of horse.

Most of them were of Irish origin and they were known as *Mary Ellens.*

It was on this visit to Bootle when I found out where my sister Jane was living. It was in two rented rooms over a cake shop in Litherland with her husband and two and a half year old daughter who I saw for the first time.

Like thousands of other families on Merseyside they were living in very poor circumstances. Arthur, her husband, was unable to find work and they were existing on the state benefit of U.A.B. (Unemployment Assistance Board). The amount of money they received each week was barely enough to keep them in food alone.

Sister Jane said truthfully she was in no position to help me as much as she would have wished to and tried to console me by pointing out I would soon be fourteen.

I barely had time to have a meal with her when mysteriously the police were on to me again.

I learned later that my brother-in-law was so afraid of being charged with harbouring me, and unable to pay a possible fine, he informed them by calling in at Bootle Town Hall. (He told me this years later). What my sister's husband could not know at that time was that within two years he, being a member of the R.N.V.R. (Royal Naval Volunteer Reserve), would be called to the colours and was fatally injured whilst serving on an aircraft carrier.

In July 1937, I donned my gym knickers for six more strokes of the birch, this was to be the last time I was to be subjected to such punishment, and it turned out to be the most spectacular.

Mr L. C. Parkes, woodwork teacher at the Home and a Heaton Moor rugby team player, was detailed to administer the strokes. He laid on the first five with his usual gusto, and, although I was bent over forward, I sensed him limbering up for the final blow (the coup de grace). In his enthusiasm his sense of direction was impaired and as a consequence, instead of the specially sprung cane landing across my buttocks, it landed low across the back of my legs. The pain was excruciating. I fell on my side on the wooden floor of the gymnasium holding the back of my legs and writhing with pain. The headmaster moved as if to assist me realizing it was a foul blow...as I looked up I caught a glimpse of Mr Parkes. He was standing there in triumph, as if he had just scored a try at rugby with an attitude of: 'That will teach you not to abscond'.

Twenty seconds or so after the blow had landed and whilst I was recovering something inside my head seemed to snap; I jumped up, in great indignation and temper, and seized the birch from his hand and struck him across the neck with it. I'm sure, if the headmaster had not been present, the fourteen stone Mr Parkes would have broken me in two pieces.

His manner towards me after the incident was one of indifference but I was never the object of his bullying again. He ignored me from then onwards although, on more than one occasion in the woodwork shop, I'd look up sharply, with a sort of sixth sense, to see him staring at me.

It was Christmas time and only eight weeks to my fourteenth birthday. I started to take stock of my life up till now.

Chapter Eight

The Royal Navy

The ever faithful Mrs Bowen continued to write to me and in her latest letter she confirmed that a home and a job were waiting for me at Appley Lock. Little did I know then what headmaster Rowe had planned for me.

In the first week of January 1938 the board of governors made one of their periodic visits to the Home. I was paraded in front of them as was the custom when a boy was due for release. I was quizzed by them about my family background, what my father did for a living, how many brothers and sisters did I have, what did they do for a living, etc., etc. Due to some of the answers I gave it must have become apparent to the panel I wasn't even aware of my family's exact whereabouts and that I never received letters from any of them only Mrs Bowen.

I was asked what I would like to do for my living when I left the Home and I replied I wanted to work with my father on the canal as all my family had done.

They asked me if I would like to join the Royal Navy to which I gave an emphatic: 'No Sir!'

At the end of the interview I was told certain enquiries would have to be made before my release, from then on I started to count the days to my freedom on my birthday.

I wrote to Mrs Bowen about my impending discharge and told her how happy I was. She wrote back saying she had written to the headmaster to confirm the preparations she had made to receive me.

On the first Monday after my fourteenth birthday events regarding my future were dropped on me like a bomb and all without any prior warning. I was awakened from my sleep in the dormitory at about 6am by Mr Arden, an hour before the usual rising time. He told me to get up, dress, and follow him downstairs. I was taken into the masters sitting room where I was told to wash at the small basin. Someone had already been to the garment room and collected my best Sunday suit, and to the locker room for my other shoes. The suit was laid over a chair as was a clean shirt, grey pullover, socks, cap, and blue gabardine raincoat. All the boys had been given clean underclothes on the Sunday morning, as was the routine. After washing, and whilst I was putting on my clean shirt, I ventured to ask Mr Arden where I was going. His reply was short and to the point: 'On a train journey'. There was no elaboration, or mention of a destination, and I found it all very puzzling.

A special treat?

I thought a nice surprise was being planned for me, as a final gesture, to make my departure a happy one. Everyone knew how much I was looking forward to going home (Hadn't I been demonstrating in a way, *prejudicial to good order and discipline* for the past three and a half years?)

But why so early in the morning, and why the secrecy?

It was usual for boys about to leave the Home for good to be informed of the fact at least a week beforehand and all the details of the event explained to them. It also gave them the opportunity to say their 'goodbyes' to the friends with whom they had lived and played with over the years and who they may never see again.

These had been occasions I had witnessed many times with sadness and envy that it hadn't been me, now I hoped it was my turn.

Some boys had said they were going to live with foster parents or to live and work on farms, others to train for a career in the Army or Royal Navy. It seemed I was not going to be given the opportunity to say goodbye to anyone.

When I was dressed and ready, Mr Arden took me into Mrs Nye's kitchen where a small table had been laid for two.

As we sat eating I dared to ask again for some information. Mr Arden said we would be going to see the headmaster at seven o'clock when all would be revealed to me. Because Mr Arden was also having an early breakfast, I deduced that wherever I was going, he was to accompany me.

We finished our meal and Mrs Nye was thanked for the special preparation. With my helping in the kitchen as a punishment, the cook knew me well. Whilst I was eating, I caught her eye once or twice, and in her occasional glances I got the impression they were tinged with sympathy. It was then I conjured up a suspicion that any surprise I was about to receive, may not be as pleasant as I was anticipating.

When we were leaving the kitchen Mrs Nye shouted to me: 'Goodbye Robert', her voice had an unmistakable tone of sadness in it as if she already knew what I was soon to find out from headmaster Rowe.

After being told to put on my gaberdine I was taken to his study. The head was standing dressed for outdoors. He at once addressed his words to me and informed me in a blunt and rather impatient manner (as if he thought it not really necessary), that I was to be taken by Mr Arden to a nautical school and there to remain for a further three years training with a view to a career in the Royal Navy!

His words didn't register in my brain for a second or two, it took me so much by surprise, but when it did, I'm sure my heart stopped beating momentarily. I was about to protest but Mr Rowe waved his arm, indicating there was no more to be said, and he was anxious that we should be on our way.

He started to walk towards the main front door where his car was parked with its engine running. He was expecting Mr Arden and myself to follow, but I would have none of it, and refused point blank to move.

I read a book in school about the press gangs that went around the taverns kidnapping boys and men and forcing them to serve in the King's Royal Navy, that was a long time ago, in about the year 1738, but this was 1938, and I thought the practice had long since ceased.

The feeling of disappointment, frustration, and fear that I felt then, would not allow me to obey, or be coaxed to comply. Mr Arden took hold of me and tried, unsuccessfully, to walk me to the car. I lay on the floor, I struggled, and I cried my protests, the noise and commotion I was making must have been heard all over the buildings.

The Rowe's housemaid came on the scene, probably thinking someone was being murdered. She was given instructions to go and fetch Mr Parkes, the *muscle man*, while Mr Arden stood over me looking quite helpless, as I lay on the floor refusing to budge.

Within minutes, *scrum half* Parkes arrived, he simply lifted me bodily from the wooden tiled floor, carried me to the waiting car and plonked me on the back seat.

A short conference took place between the three masters then Mr Parkes hurried away to reappear ten minutes later carrying his overcoat.

It was intended that Mr Arden would take me the two hundred miles journey to the Wellesley Nautical School, Blyth, Northumberland, on his own; but on reflection, the head realized he would need some assistance and so Mr Parkes was detailed to accompany us all the way. A little later than originally planned, we all four of us set off in the car bound for Manchester.

We stopped in the precincts of the London & North Eastern Railway station, where Mr Rowe pulled out his wallet and handed Mr Parkes money; he promptly went to the booking office to purchase a return ticket for himself while we remained in the car.

On his return, we all proceeded to the platform where the train for Newcastle-Upon-Tyne was already standing and about to depart. Mr Parkes kept a vice-like grip on my gaberdine coat collar as we were walking across the station. I remember getting the urge to shout out to the people on the station that I was being *taken against my will*, but I had second thoughts about this course of action in case they had me certified as insane.

We boarded the train, Mr Rowe seeing us seated in the carriage. Despite all the trouble I had caused him over the past three years he wished me well, and expressed the hope I would like the nautical school, (some hope!) then he was gone, out of my life for ever. (Years later I read he died from a heart attack while attending a headmasters' conference in Birmingham in 1942, he was aged 62).

On reflection I have no bitter memories of Mr Rowe, he was I believe a good man with a difficult job on occasions which he handled with some considerable kindness.

The train sped northwards through Yorkshire stopping at Leeds to pick up more passengers and water for the locomotive. It later stopped at Thirsk, Darlington, and Durham, before pulling into Newcastle.

As we travelled north I made a mental note of the stations beyond Leeds. because the latter city would be my main objective to return to when I *got off* this training ship and made my way south again.

I would be seeking the sanctuary of the Leeds and Liverpool Canal once more. I began to realize it was a long way back to Manchester and still further to Bootle.

I was feeling very dejected and dismayed knowing that if I succeeded in making it back to Leeds it was still another 124 miles along the waterway to Merseyside.

We eventually boarded a small suburban train to Blyth.

The two masters hadn't a lot to say to me during the journey they were too busy trying to impress each other, Mr Arden being an academic, while Mr Parkes was more brawn than brain.

Because of these new and unexpected developments, instead of all my troubles coming to an end, it now seemed to me as if it was going to start all over again, for a further three years with lots more punishment in store for me.

I felt a real sense of injustice at what was happening to me and also that it was illegal. I had not been to any court which had decreed I should spend three years in a nautical school, and I certainly had never expressed a wish to do so. I was to be forced into one of the armed forces as were many boys from homes and orphanages all over England and Wales, Scotland had their own laws.

We arrived at the Training Ship Wellesley which had gates instead of a gangway. The first thing I noticed just inside the gate was a tall white pole with a flag at the top. It was a mock up of a ship's mast complete with two rope ladders and a crows nest. Beyond it was a cluster of wooden huts, surrounded by fields, with not a drop of water in sight. Water was close by, further to the east, but it was over the perimeter and out of bounds, on the North East coast.

The first hut inside the entrance I imagine would be the guard house; I don't know for sure because I wasn't in the establishment long enough to find out. Outside the guard house hung a ship's brass bell, complete with a white rope dangling from it, and as you got closer you could read the words 'T.S. Wellesley' stamped on it.

Interview with the Captain

Messrs Arden, Parkes, and myself, were ushered into the captain's quarters. He was seated behind a desk and dressed in the uniform of a R.N.V.R. four ringed captain. Mr Arden handed him the papers appertaining to my pedigree.

Before studying them closely and anticipating the two masters were anxious to be away because of the timing of the trains back to Newcastle, a signature was obtained for my body and the meeting was quickly over and so Arden and Parkes went out of my life.

Strangely, as soon as they'd gone I felt I'd been abandoned and left with an alien dressed as a human. For the very first time I wished I was back at Barnes Home.

In my three and a half years at Heaton Mersey, I had become one of the oldest and long established senior boys in the Home, familiar with everything and everyone, now I was very junior, being forced to wear an uncommon form of dress, and expected to learn a different expression of the English language, giving objects other names.

I realized I was certainly out of the frying pan and into the fire.

I was left standing on front of the head of the nautical school, not allowing myself the time to find out what his name was.

Another officer came into the *hut ward room*, this *bloke* had three gold rings on his arm, and stood at the captain's side.

In those days such officers were considered far superior than they are today. Today they just get more money! The commanding officer was absorbed in reading the papers given to him by Mr Arden, whilst doing so he looked up at me occasionally, with some disbelief, as if he couldn't believe what he was reading, with his gold rimmed spectacles that matched the gold braid.

He eventually spoke to me to ask: 'Why do you want to join the Navy?' He was very surprised when I told him I had no wish to do so.

I was sharply reminded to stand to attention in the presence of the *Skipper* by t'other fella with three stripes.

I was then asked what I wanted to do in order to earn my living when I left the ship? I replied: 'I'm going to work on the Leeds & Liverpool Canal with my father'. My answer brought a whimsical smile to both officers faces as if I'd said something funny.

Still reading the report from Barnes Home the captain remarked: 'I gather you were an habitual absconder? To which I made no reply (I pretended not to understand the word habitual). He went on to say: 'You will find there are no walls or bars here to stop you going A.W.O.L., but we do have the cure for "deserters"'... He didn't elaborate or describe the cure.

I knew the punishment of keel hauling was no longer legal and there was no water under this *ship* anyway!

I was questioned about the type of punishment I received at the Home, and how many times I'd received it. He looked a little surprised and dismayed when I told him. His final comment was: 'Perhaps they didn't lay it on hard enough'.

The interrogation came to an end, and a leading rating was sent for. He was a six-feet tall youth of about sixteen years old and looked frightened to death in the presence of the two officers. He was ordered to take me to the ship's stores, to be fitted up with a sailors' uniform.

The Royal Navy garb for the lower deck personnel was designed about two hundred years ago and is not in my opinion a practical outfit; what purpose do wide bell bottomed trousers have, except to maybe trip over when climbing the rigging, or flap about whilst doing the sailors hornpipe?

Then there's the top part of the uniform, the tight fitting garment with the feminine name, *the blouse*, which you could just be struggling into as the enemy is attacking.

The silly collar, which fits like a babies' bib in reverse; the rounded cap with no brim or peak, to protect your eyes from the wind and rain, or the sun. I thought the piece of white cotton rope that fits around the neck and under the bib, known as the lanyard, could be a means of ending it all when you could no longer stand the the arrogance and smugness of the so called *well bred* officers or if you were about to receive twenty lashes of the cat of nine tails while roped to the main mast.

The Royal Navy was all about tradition and class discrimination. I consider the greatest sailor that ever lived was Captain James Cook, a Yorkshireman, the Admiralty argued long and hard before making him a captain, because it was considered he was not well bred enough, and coming from Whitby of all places.

Kitting and breaking out

As I was drawing my gear I would have preferred a nice cut suit like the captains, without the gold braid of course, instead I was fitted up with a *Battle of Trafalgar* effort.

After collecting all the gear I was entitled to I was taken to my allotted mess instead of belonging to a house, the mess was called *Grenville* after some aristocratic admiral.

I was shown where to *stow* the surplus wearing apparel. After struggling into my sailors suit I was now ready to learn to dance the hornpipe. The rating, (I didn't know what rating he was) who had been taking me around was impatient to be away to mix with his *oppoes*, so he left me to find my own sea legs.

Before he left me, he mentioned something about eight bells, four bells, reveille, out pipes, and goodness knows what. He also recommended that if I wanted to know anything more about anything else, to ask one of the other blokes.

The only thing I really wanted to know was the time of the next train from Newcastle-Upon-Tyne to Liverpool.

I managed to find my way to the dining hall, galley on board. As well as filling my stomach at the evening meal, I also filled the pockets of my new greatcoat with left-over bread in preparation for the trek south to Lancashire.

By now it was beginning to go dusk and a ground frost was settling over the fields that surrounded the huts. The ratings who had been walking around had now gone inside for warmth.

I was wearing a new pair of boots that were soon to be well and truly broken in. It had been some time since I'd worn boots, it had been shoes for the past three and a half years, and mostly bare feet before then.

When the darkness deepened, lights from the roadways shone by each hut and from the windows. There were a few shadowy figures moving in and out of the *messes* as I hid in the dark until I thought the coast was clear, then I hurriedly made my way towards the perimeter of the *ship* and through a gap in the hedge, which I had already earmarked, and across adjoining fields in the direction of Blyth. I was on my way to Bootle once again.

The total time I spent at the Wellesley Nautical School was six hours out of the intended three years.

Since travelling from the railway station that day I still had a mental recollection of its locality. As I came onto the public highway I attempted to keep in the shadows, especially when vehicles approached me from each direction.

As I got closer to the station I was alerted when I saw the figure of a policeman, clad in a waterproof cape, leaning on his bicycle, talking to a railway porter under the glow of a gas lamp at the entrance.

Three hours or so must have passed since I *abandoned* ship, and I assumed I had been found to be missing and the police had been asked to keep a look out for me, likewise the railway staff. I made a quick turn around, wanting to get off the public thoroughfare altogether, I walked into a goods siding. It was sparsely lit, but I could see it was full of coal wagons, and was a very miserable place to be on a cold winter's night. I was thankful for the Navy greatcoat I was wearing.

I felt wretched as I stood on one spot among the wagons hopping from one foot to the other attempting to keep warm. I moved to a place in the siding where I could see the station platform. Everything was quiet and still save for the occasional passing of a vehicle on the road.

By now I'd lost all idea of time. Two passenger trains consisting of only two carriages each stopped at the station, one was travelling north, in the direction of Berwick-on-Tweed and the Scottish border, the other was proceeding south to Newcastle, my next intended destination.

From where I stood I could hear the sound of carriage doors being slammed, and could see the trains pulling out of the station. The slits of light coming from the carriage windows looked warm and inviting but I made no attempt to get on to the platform. I thought it wiser to wait until the first sign of activity in the early hours of the morning, when I assumed a different shift of railway porters would be on duty, and the powers that wanted me would think I would be miles away by that time.

As I kept peering at the station platform I pictured a waiting room maybe with a burning coal fire. My dark blue Naval raincoat had started to turn white with the hoar frost.

Soon after the departure of the last train a porter began to walk the length of the platform, carrying a pole on his shoulder. With it he put out most of the gas lamps by pulling down one of the hanging chains to cut off the gas supply. He left those at the ends continuing to burn brightly. Even just to look at them made me feel a bit warmer. It seemed there would not be any more trains going anywhere that night, and my thoughts turned to finding somewhere a little more comfortable and warmer than standing in the sidings all night so I cautiously ventured nearer to the platform.

None of the rooms on the station had any lights lit and I could see the entrance had been locked. Tiptoeing along the platform proper, not daring to make a sound in case the porter might still be on the premises, I tried the door marked *Waiting Room* but it was locked as were all the others. I finally settled down in what had become over the years one of my most frequent places to rest and avoid people, the gentlemen's lavatory.

I sat on a toilet seat with arms folded, the collar of the greatcoat turned up, and with my head partially buried in the lapels trying to get some warmth from my own breath. Sitting in that toilet was like enjoying the comforts of home compared to standing in the goods yard. Although I dozed a little I couldn't sleep.

The standard of cleanliness and hygiene in public lavatories in those days, though a bit more primitive, was higher than it is today and there was plenty more of them available.

It was some hours later, and still dark, when I was alerted by footsteps on the platform and the rattling of keys as doors were being unlocked. Someone came into the toilet to use the *standing stone* and I sat very quiet. As the minutes went by there were more footsteps. I guessed these were intending passengers for the first train due in, so I made preparations to be one of them, by making sure my bell-bottomed trousers were well tucked in my socks, and buttoning up my greatcoat at the neck in an endeavour to hide the uniform underneath. I just wished then I'd had a cloth cap to don, as befitted all working class men of that time.

Back on the rails

Soon a train entered the station, and I strode out on to the platform to join about a dozen men waiting. They were miners going to work on the early morning shift. Besides wearing pit helmets and heavy boots, around their waists they wore thick leather belts, with *snap tins* and tea cans hanging from them. Their trousers were tied with string just below the knee (to make bending easier whilst they were underground). The pieces of string hitching their pants up were known as *bow-yanks*.

When I arrived on the platform seemingly from nowhere, I became the object of some curious glances right away and more so when I inquired from one of them if the train now coming in went to Newcastle.

The reply came in a strong affirmative Geordie accent of 'Wi I man', and a look of great surprise on his face at me not knowing. The accent was the same as one of my pals at Barnes Home, John Marshall, he came from Wallsend-on-Tyne and I'd been listening to him for three years.

When the train came to a halt the colliers climbed into two carriages, while I got into one on my own hoping not to be observed by the porter. I gave a sigh of relief when the train pulled out of the station, at least I was leaving Blyth, how far I got depended on luck, sense of direction, and my initiative.

In the 1930s most manual workers started the working day at 7am, and a basic working week, which included four hours on Saturday, was approximately 50 hours.

The train stopped at a couple of small stations before it arrived in Newcastle. It was now about 7am on the Tuesday, just twenty four hours since being forced into a car at Heaton Mersey. It had been the longest day in my life. Already the main line station was bustling with people and this was to my liking as it made me feel less conspicuous.

As I stepped off the train I thought, 'so far so good', then my thoughts turned to my stomach, it was empty again, I'd eaten all the bread stuffed in my pockets and I didn't know where the next meal was coming from. How I longed for the cultivated fields of South-west Lancashire that flourished alongside the canal where I could always alleviate the hunger pangs.

I had no trouble getting from one platform to another via iron bridges, and after consulting timetables at which I had become an expert, I learnt that I'd not long missed a train to Manchester via Leeds, and the next one was in two hours time.

Author 'Bob Buck Ranty' Houghton steering 'Progress' towards
Downholland Bridge, Ormskirk, 1942.

My first priority was to find something to eat; I was rewarded after
scavenging in the pig bins, outside the station tea rooms at the rear of
the buildings, where I found an abundance of stale loaves of bread.
After eating my fill, I wrapped some in newspaper for times ahead.

To see people rooting in bins in that day and age, was not an uncommon sight. The reason I was so fortunate that morning was probably because I was the first there. The many tramps on the road were forever
stealing from the pigs.

I boarded a train bound for Manchester at 9.30am and took up my
stance in the corridor in the centre of the carriage, a position I knew
from past experience to be the most advantageous.

The train pulled out and the first stop was Durham which proved to
be an uneventful first leg, so to speak, but as it proceeded to its next
scheduled stop, I heard the dreaded shout of 'All Tickets Please', as the

inspector slid open the compartment doors in the next carriage. I made a quick retreat into the toilet and locked myself in.

I could hear the snip of his clippers in the compartment next to the toilet as I sat and waited for the expected rattle of the lavatory door handle, but there was no rattle, and all went quiet once more. The inspector had passed by either without bothering or an oversight. I got to know through experience that some inspectors were more conscientious at their job than others. Some, if they saw a lavatory door showing the *engaged* sign on as they came to it, they would rattle like mad, and wait for the occupant to respond to their command, others were in a hurry to complete the task and just passed by. Lucky for me, it was one of the latter on this day.

The train stopped at Darlington, Northallerton, and Thirsk, the next stop was Leeds City.

By now the strain of standing in the corridor keeping a constant vigilance for ticket inspectors was becoming too much of a worry. I had never covered so many illicit miles on a train before and I decided to embark when we reached Leeds.

Like Liverpool, and more especially Bootle, Leeds had a familiar sound to its name for me because the canal joined the two cities together. To people not associated with it, it was just another canal, but to me, even then, and more so now, it means a lot more.

It has a two hundred year history, and in that time, many of its bargees

Canal Transport's Manchester Road Depot, Burnley, 1910.

were born on it. Quite a number of them were my ancestors, born in the cabins of the hundreds of boats that plied the waterway. Their births attended by other boatmen's wives, who helped in the deliveries. I was told that some of the births were never registered, which made it difficult for them in later life, when they came up against officialdom requiring documents, for pension applications, etc.

Boat boys started to help work the boat when they were as young as five, and never attended any school until it was made compulsory. In the 1930s approximately 90% of the older boatmen were totally illiterate.

My own parents and grandparents were an example. My great great grandfather was a boatman on the Leeds and Liverpool canal, born at Halsall in West Lancashire in 1799, where the first sod was cut at the start of the canal's construction.

Boatmen worked according to the daylight hours or availability of movement due to weather, like ice, or if they considered the horse had done enough pulling. The horse was an important part of the team which made their livelihood possible, so it was given a great deal of consideration.

A number of boatmen who suffered bad health prematurely usually finished their days in one of the many workhouses near the canal's route, and then on to a pauper's grave. The workhouses served more than one purpose, it was a shelter for the elderly, poor and destitute, the sick, and also the mentaly retarded.

The construction of the workhouses was similar in design to that of prisons with the same forbidding walls and morbid buildings—but I digress.

By 4 o'clock in the afternoon that Tuesday I had successfully negotiated the ticket barrier and was walking the streets of Leeds, en route for the canal towpath. When I arrived at Leeds Wharf Office, the milestone read Liverpool 127 miles.

Walking from Leeds I came to Apperley Lock in Yorkshire, not to be confused with Appley Lock, near Wigan in Lancashire.

Uncomfortable Quarters

It was quite dark, with a frosty moon shining brightly, when I approached one of the many humpty-backed stone bridges which joined a narrow road, sometimes little more than a cart track, which seemingly coming and going nowhere. By the side of the track and close to the bridge stood a discoloured, once whitewashed derelict

The derelict cottage in Yorkshire where I spent a night when A.W.O.L from Wellesly Nautical School, Northumberland, 1938.

cottage. With half of its roof fallen inside its four walls it looked like it had been abandoned long ago.

It was time for me to be looking for somewhere to rest for the night, so I climbed the steep grassy slope, leading from the bank to the cottage, to have a look for possible shelter.

The ruin did not have doors and there wasn't any glass in the window frames. Inside it was overgrown with weeds and piled with rubble. There was however a small part in one corner where the roof was still intact and appeared safe from collapse, which offered some little protection from the elements. Lying flat on the floor was one of the cottage doors, so I moved it under the roof, then I lay down on it to rest, curling myself into a ball for warmth.

It was a very cold night making sleep on the hard door out of the question and to add to this discomfort, there was the constant rustling sounds made by nocturnal animals, perhaps rats. Whenever the sounds came closer I made a sound and moved myself, to frighten them away. Once during the night I heard the sound of a motor boat's engine. Through the hole in the roof of the cottage I could see the sky lit up by the boat's bow headlight. For a few seconds the noise changed, as it passed under the bridge, which caused an echo from the walls below me. For a few brief moments I felt comfort from a bit of human company. The boat sailed on and the sound of its engine grew fainter then all was quiet again.

While I was lying, on what could have once been the front door of the cottage I began to picture the faces of some of my pals in Barnes Home. I imagined them all to be tucked up in their nice warm beds in the dormitories. I had the added sadness that I would never see any of them again now I was no longer a Barnes Home boy.

Tom Carrington ('Tommy-Nine-Toes') and wife 'tied up' at Burscough Bridge. (Tommy lost a toe when his horse trod on him).

Chapter Nine

Reminiscing

When you attend an ordinary day school, from 9am to 4pm, your school friends are also your neighbours, who play out in the streets with you in the evenings, and even after you leave school you continue to associate, and in fact, see each other grow up. Sadly that wasn't to be my lot, or one of my future memories.

Even today, after all the years have gone by, those young faces I had to leave behind in the Home remain in my memory. I often wonder how they fared in their lives, and where they are now. No doubt some will be scattered to all parts of the world and like me they will be fathers and grandfathers, but *they shall not grow old* in my memory.

My thoughts also set me wondering about the inhabitants that had once lived in the cottage, and I imagined them sitting around the fire on just such a cold winter's night as this. Such thoughts helped to pass the time away.

I was glad when daylight broke so I could stretch my legs and be on my way; lying on the hard door had made my joints stiff. I eventually scrambled down the slope and onto the bank continuing my marathon walk through Yorkshire and Lancashire.

For my breakfast I had the usual diet when I was on the run, raw turnip. During this *safari* I realized I had to discard the sailors' uniform and acquire civilian clothes before I could look for work now I was turned fourteen. My dilemma was where was I going to get the clothes from? I kept thinking of the problem as I walked, and felt confident I'd somehow find the solution.

There was plenty of canal traffic on the move throughout the day to capture my interest. All the boats were gaily painted and had scrubbed white cotton rope fenders hanging over their sides. The 'piece de resistance' was always the intricate Turks Head right on the front, hanging from the main bow stem timber, each crew trying to outdo each other for style, and all with pride.

The cargoes of coal were not covered but other merchandise such as sugar, grain, cotton bales, and machinery, all had tarpaulin sheets covering them. The sheeting was shaped like a long black tent, stretching from stem to stern, with the company's name printed in white capital letters. It was seeing *Canal Transport Ltd. Pall Mall. Liverpool* printed on the covers that decided me to apply for a job with them as a barge mate.

As I walked I hardly noticed the miles passing by, because every minute I was free was a pleasure to me. I walked for fourteen hours that day, still living off the produce in the fields and begging water from wayside cottages.

I passed through Shipley and Bingley, where I saw the Bingley Five Rise Lock for the first time. I stopped for a while observing the boatmen as they worked the boats through the locks, all crews, including those waiting their turn to enter, helping each other. Once or twice I gave a hand, by helping to shove open, or close the lock gates. This action was usually responded to, with being asked, in the boatmen's own vernacular: 'How go little mate. Arta all reet?'

Bingley Five Rise Locks, Yorkshire.

I continued on through Silsden, Skipton, and Barnoldswick, and as the light began to fade, I came to Foulridge Tunnel. Here the towpath came to an abrupt end, and the canal went underground.

I walked overland, as do the horses, before resuming the path at the other end and in doing so I had crossed the border from Yorkshire into Lancashire.

When horse boats come to the tunnel, after unhitching the horse, the boats have to be *legged* through the tunnel by lying on your back and putting your feet in the holes in the side of the tunnel, which had been especially constructed for that very purpose.

I could now see the lights of Nelson, a mill town where I was hoping to find a warm dry shelter for the night.

When I started off from Apperley Lock that morning, the canal milestone read 118 miles to Liverpool, at Nelson it was down to 89 miles. I knew the milestone at Wigan Pier read 35 miles and I thought, with a little extra effort, I might make it to Wigan the following night.

It was Wednesday evening and 48 hours since I'd left Northumberland, I told myself at least I'm back in Lancashire again, and that was good for my morale.

During my travels on the waterway I noticed quite a number of boatmen, especially those manning the diesel-engined ones, carried a bicycle of sorts with them, this was usually kept at the stern end, ready to jump off with. I said of sorts, because most of the bikes consisted only of wheels on a frame, with a saddle and handlebars and with none of the other fixtures and fittings. They were used for riding on the towpath ahead of the boat, to turn off the many wooden swing bridges, and to turn them on again once the boat had passed through. They were also used to make a lock ready, by the time a vessel reached it, minimising the delay in waiting for the level of water to rise or fall, depending on whether you're going up or down the lock.

A bike was also handy for nipping down a country lane to an isolated shop for a loaf of bread, or to a farmhouse to purchase a piece of home-cured bacon, eggs, a lump of pork or other produce. A bicycle was a very useful accessory and it started me thinking it would be very advantageous to me if I had one.

I had also thought of a place where I might obtain a suit of clothes. At first I thought the idea too audacious, but as I couldn't think of anywhere else, my mind kept going back to it. Desperate straits brought on desperate measures.

My plan was to make my way to Heaton Mersey and to Barnes Home, then break into the storeroom where all the clothes were kept; one hundred and eighty suits, and the same number of gaberdine raincoats were hanging in unlocked cupboards.

Changing direction to reach Heaton Mersey would mean making a considerable detour and the answer to that was a bicycle, so I decided to steal one. All the times I'd absconded from Barnes Home, the only thing I had ever stolen were rides on trains or produce from farmers fields, but now with the threat of spending another three years incarcerated in Northumberland, which I thought unjust, I had a feeling of desperation.

Obtaining own transport

Darkness had fallen by the time I was walking through Nelson town centre, and those inhabitants who were not inside their houses, listening to the wireless, were making their way to the pictures or the pubs for an evening's entertainment.

Bicycles were ridden in greater numbers than they are today. The main reason for their decline is the volume of traffic on the roads moving a lot faster and with little consideration for the bike rider. I for one don't like buses overtaking me and missing me by about six or seven inches.

I roamed Nelson for two hours before I finally found a cycle. It had a small enough frame from which I could reach the pedals. It had been left outside a public house, and when I grabbed hold of it I walked it along the road towards the canal, making no attempt to ride, but content just to get it onto the towpath. It was too dark to ride on the canal side, and with walking all that day, I did not have enough energy to push the pedals. After walking the machine a short distance, I came to some uninhabited boats moored on the opposite side of the canal. By crossing a bridge to get to them and after closer inspection, I found an unfurnished cabin with benches in it to rest on.

I placed the bike in the empty hold of the boat, then clambered down into the cold but dry cabin, partially replacing the square wooden scuttle cover to keep out the cold nighr air, before stretching out on the bench to rest my aching limbs.

I still had a piece of turnip in my overcoat pocket, which I ate for my supper. But I hadn't had a hot drink for two days and three nights, how I longed for a mug of hot tea.

During the night two motor boats went by, their movement causing a wash which made the tied-up boats strain at the moorings and bump against the coping stones which fortified the banks of the canal. Not having any idea of the time I kept getting up from the bench throughout the night to peer out of the scuttle hole to see if there was any sign of the dawn.

Further along the bank I could see a large mill with its hundreds of small windows lit up; from inside came the sound of the weaving looms working a night shift spinning cotton. Later in my life I got to know the mill as *Brierfield*, and subsequently I passed by it on hundreds of occasions in earning my living as the captain of a motor boat belonging to Canal Transport Ltd.

The 'Wharfe' jammed between lock gates; caused by a piece of driftwood wedged behind the gate.

The darkness began to lift, and as dawn approached I was anxious to be astride the bike, I didn't want to be found in the boat's cabin, trespassing, with a stolen bicycle in the hold.

It was a cold and frosty morning, and there was a thin layer of ice on the water when I jumped out of the cabin and mounted the two wheels. I felt the cold intensely, especially on my face, when I first started off, but after a short time my whole body warmed up, as I pedalled with gusto. I was another five miles further on, and nearing Burnley, when literally dozens of people, mostly women, were on the towpath. They were mill hands taking a short cut to their place of work.

I dismounted and stood holding the bike to let them pass by me, and getting a few curious looks from some of them as they passed by.

I passed the Canal Transport Burnley warehouse, where a number of their craft were tied up alongside the sheds. Men were already at work unloading large bales of cotton from one of them. The cotton would have been brought to Liverpool by ship, then by horse and cart to a canal warehouse wharf.

On a quieter stretch of the canal bank, I stopped to have a closer look at the bike. It was a Raleigh model, not new, but in good condition. There was a pump attached to the frame, and it was fitted with dynamo lighting, front and rear. Behind the seat, and hanging from it, was a small leather pouch. On opening it, I found it contained spanners and a repair outfit. With one of the spanners I adjusted the saddle to a lower position, so that my short legs reached the pedals more firmly making riding more comfortable. This done, I remounted and continued on my way.

One of the advantages of riding a bicycle on a canal towpath is that you're always riding on a level, there are no hills to climb, traffic lights, or road junctions, and no other traffic, except boat horses. In a small way, it compensates for the extra miles entailed when travelling the waterway route.

In the centre of the towpath there is always a narrow smooth *inner path*, this is made by the horses who plod along it. They make it by design and instinct, to avoid the sharp stones that make their feet sore.

The disadvantage is having to dismount at the numerous low and narrow stone bridges, for fear of banging your head as you go under them, and possibly finishing up in the water.

Pedalling at a moderate pace, I was now covering distance three times faster than on foot, and passing the metal milestones that much quicker.

I made a brief stop at Clayton-Le-Moors to beg a cup of water, and by mid-day I was in Blackburn.

Because I was making such good progress, the possibility of reaching Heaton Mersey by that evening to plunder a civilian suit of clothes and a raincoat, had now become more of a reality.

Being able to memorize the geography of Lancashire from classroom maps, I knew it would be a lot nearer, therefore quicker, to leave the canal side at Blackburn and proceed via the public highway to Manchester through Bolton, and this I did.

Beyond Bolton and approaching Tyldesley, I came to the Wigan Road, and the route I used to take when walking from Manchester to Wigan, so now I was on familiar roads, and knew exactly where I was.

It was rush hour when I reached Salford, with thousands of people making their way home from work. With the traffic being so dense, I walked the bike on the pavement through the centre of Manchester along Deansgate, Piccadilly, and so on to Stockport Road at Ardwick.

I was less than five miles from Barnes Home and it was Thursday evening. I couldn't help thinking how surprised Mr Rowe would be if he had known I was approaching his domain with the sole intent of burglary and larceny.

Breaking in, not out

For the first time and after more than three years of breaking out of his establishment, I was now hell bent on breaking in.

It had seemed a long time since the previous Monday when he had dispatched me poste haste to a place I considered more distant than the North Pole.

It was dark as I walked along the gas-lit Stockport Road, through Leverhulme and Longsight, with their abundance of second-hand shops, most of which had closed for the day. There were still a few general corner shops open, and would remain so until late on in the evening.

My legs felt like two lumps of lead, and looking in the windows of food shops only increased my hunger.

Being very knowledgeable with the routine and general layout of Barnes Home, I anticipated not only helping myself to a suit of clothes and a raincoat, but also some food from Mrs Nye's kitchen.

I walked the remainder of the way to Heaton Mersey instead of riding, for two reasons, firstly I was too weak to ride, and also to time my arrival for around 10pm. By then the boys would have washed, had their supper of powdered milk, with the hard round biscuit, and the dormitory lights would have been switched off.

I could never have imagined that only a week previously, when I was actually looking forward to leaving the Home legitimately, that within a matter of days I would be dressed in a sailor suit breaking back in.

When I arrived there were a few lighted windows in the staff quarters. I deposited the bike out of sight, behind a hedge on the perimeter of the gardens before crossing them on foot, then I stood in the shadow of the buildings where I couldn't be seen from the roadway, or from the large private houses in the vicinity.

I was standing close to the window, which I knew was the cloakroom, where the boys' suits and raincoats were hanging in wardrobes, in numerical order. I watched and waited until all the lights in the staff quarters were out, leaving everywhere in darkness.

I cracked one of the small panes of glass by the catch, with a stone held in my hand. Making as little noise as possible, I removed the whole pane and picked out the pieces one at a time which enabled me to put my hand through, release the lock, and slide the window open.

I climbed inside, and although there was very little light, being familiar with the interior, it didn't take me long to pick out a suit and a raincoat my size, and put them on.

I felt better as soon as I was dressed in civilian clothes instead of the silly sailor suit. I was once again in short trousers. I sat on the wooden floor, resting my back on the wall, and using the Navy greatcoat to keep my legs warm, considering my next move.

I had second thoughts of attempting to get into the kitchen for food. So far things had gone according to plan, and I didn't want to push my luck. I thought I would acquire a second raincoat, and wear them both at the same time, until an opportunity came to sell one of them in a second-hand shop for money to buy some food.

I sat in the cloakroom resting and waiting for the first signs it was time for me to be on my way. When I started to hear the noises of motor vehicles and the clip clop of horses shoes as they pulled the carts to Stockport Market, I took that as a sign for me to leave even though it was still dark.

Climbing back through the window, I walked across the gardens to retrieve the bike. After connecting the small wheel of the dynamo to press against the rear tyre to make the lighting work, I set off in the direction of Wellington Road North, and Manchester.

As I rode along, I wondered about the wisdom of leaving the sailors' uniform and the greatcoat on the floor of the cloakroom. When the break-in was reported to the police, and the clothes with my name stamped inside were found, the identity of the burglar would be realized.

What a shock it would be for headmaster Rowe and his staff when he learnt it was I, once numbered 2 in the Home, that was responsible for the break-in. I now had a suit belonging to boy number 47, and his raincoat, and another raincoat. I've often wondered what their reaction and comments had been when they discovered my outrageous return.

As I neared Manchester city centre, again I preferred to walk, rather than compete with the traffic and the tram lines, the latter being to my mind a cyclists nightmare.

I crossed a bridge over the River Irwell and I was now in the City of Salford. As I travelled, I kept looking for second-hand shops. At the first attempt a dealer gave me three shillings for the raincoat. It was worth a lot more but he was eager to make a nice profit, and I was hungry.

A bit further on, in Eccles, I bought a small fresh crusty loaf and a bottle of lemonade and sat on a road side seat, eating and drinking.

I was feeling in high spirits as I continued astride the bike, and full of happy expectations, especially after getting rid of the uniform, and because I was on the last lap of my journey to Liverpool.

So much had happened since the previous Monday morning, that I could hardly believe that it was now only Friday.

I anticipated that as more days went by the search for me would intensify and after finding the discarded uniform at Heaton Mersey, the people looking for me would know where to look. For this reason I decided to quit the public highway and retreat back to the watery route of my ancestors.

Back on the canal

At Eccles I got onto the Bridgewater Canal, and followed it through to Leigh, a distance of eight miles via Worsley and Boothstown.

At Leigh the Bridgewater Canal then becomes the Leeds and Liverpool and a further eight miles on is Wigan Pier.

My mind was constantly engaged in thinking what was the best strategy to avoid capture and being sent back to T.S. Wellesley.

I thought of the possible consequences of being apprehended in possession of the stolen bicycle and being found guilty of burglary, theft, and of defrauding the L.N.E.R. Railway, between Blyth and Leeds.

I had heard of Borstal Institutions, and from what I'd been told, they were pretty difficult places to escape from, because of all the bolts and bars, more in fact than I'd ever encountered at Barnes Home.

It was being able to get out, rather than any punishment inflicted, which worried me most of all. I had learned to take punishment, but I couldn't cope with being locked away.

I thought to get rid of the bike, just as soon as I reached Wigan. My first thought was to abandon it in the street, with a note saying it had been stolen in Nelson, that way the owner might recover it, but that was not to happen.

I had no intention of calling at Appley Lock Cottages to see Mrs Bowen and old Tom, as much as I would have liked to see them again after nine months. I wondered if they had been told of my transfer to Northumberland? One thing was certain, it was too far away for her to visit me there.

My main desire was to reach Liverpool, and seek a job as a barge mate. I thought if I started work, the powers with authority over me might let me continue at it, which would be better for all concerned.

The authors father 'Dick Ranty' Houghton unloading manure at Tarleton.

Before applying at the Canal Transport offices, I would have to look the part, and be ready to start immediately if required.

Working clothes

I couldn't go to work in short trousers; the very least I required was a pair of working men's overalls, and few of the working class went without a cloth cap on their heads.

These things cost money, and all I had was a few pennies left over from the sale of the raincoat. This necessity is what started me thinking to try to sell the bike, rather than just to abandoned it in the street. It had served one very good purpose, it could now serve another, by providing me with some badly needed money.

I arrived in the outskirts of Wigan in the early afternoon of Friday and for a short time I sat and rested at Pagefield Locks, eating chips wrapped in newspaper.

From Pagefield I pushed the bike to Wigan open market, again I was on the lookout for second-hand shops on the way. At the market I stopped to look at the wares hanging upon one particular stall. The items that caught my eye were bib and brace overalls, and working mens union shirts, as they were called. As I stood looking at them, the man in attendance suddenly asked: 'Can I help thee lad?' in his broad Lancashire accent.

I remember replying, telling him that I'd just left school and was hoping to start work soon, and for that reason I would be requiring a pair of overalls and shirt, but first I would have to sell the bike to raise the money to pay for them.

I could see by the expression on his face that he was somewhat taken aback by my statement. Then he asked: 'Where does thar live lad?' I replied 'Appley Bridge', and with that I made to walk away from the stall. I thought he was becoming too inquisitive, and might in fact put two and two together, and call a policeman. (There was invariably one on hand in those days) He shouted: 'How much does thar waant fort bike?' I retraced my steps, and after some verbal bartering, we came to an agreement.

I told the stall-holder it would be with my father's approval, if he gave me a pair of overalls, a shirt, and five shillings, he could have the bike. The market man took the bike from me and placed it behind his stall, he then proceeded to make a parcel of the clothes.

The parcel was handed to me, together with the five shillings. He wished me luck in my first job, and with that, I legged it up the road as fast as I could, feeling very pleased with myself, and very rich.

I opened the parcel in one of the few places available to me for a bit of privacy, a cubicle in the public lavatories in the market.

After putting on the long legged overalls, over my short trousers, and replacing the naval-type shirt with the new one, I left the public conveniences and went into a cheap looking cafe and bought bacon sandwiches and tea. While I was sitting in the cocoa rooms in King Street I realized I hadn't got a cap, so after leaving the cafe, I went into a gentlemen's outfitters and acquired my first cloth cap for one shilling and nine pence (8p). I remember the shop very well because it was next door to the Wigan Hippodrome Music Hall in King Street.

Now that I was suitably attired to do a days work, hopefully years, my thoughts turned to applying for a job.

It was now too late on in the day for such a venture so I decided to leave the quest until the following morning. The next day was Saturday when almost everybody worked until 12 noon.

Around 5pm there was a clatter of clogs on the pavements as the hundreds of mill hands left work to make their way home, the women and young girls linking each other and chatting merrily as they walked.

Lancashire and Yorkshire mill folk were a happy and carefree breed of people. Although they did not receive a great amount of payment for the laborious and repetitive work, and the long hours, they always seemed to be in a happy frame of mind, ready to help one another.

In another hour it would be dark again, already the cold February night air was descending on the fifth night I had to endure without a bed to go to, but I was still feeling very optimistic.

I spent another hour sitting in a cafe keeping warm and drinking hot tea, purchased with my ill-gotten gains, and decided to spend the evening on a visit to the Hippodrome where the entertainment commenced at 6.30.

For the next three hours my mind was taken off the unpleasant happenings and circumstances in my life by the singing, dancing, and the laughter. It was lovely to sit in the warmth of the theatre high up in the gallery. I could have spent the entire night in there but, alas, the final curtain came down signalling the end of the show. The National Anthem was played as we stood to attention and then it was out into the cold frosty streets once again.

The 'Water Witch'; used for transporting executives on inspection tours.

I went into the first of the many fish and chip shops and waited my turn to buy my supper.

Most people on the streets were making their way home to warm fires, and warm beds, some were waiting for public transport to take them there. I needed to find shelter fairly quickly as it neared 11pm. I didn't want to be on the streets much later, for fear of being spotted, and maybe stopped by one of the all night foot patrolling policemen.

I made my way up King Street and across Wallgate to the market place where I'd been earlier in the day, now it was deserted. I made use of some canvas sheeting and, out of sight of would-be patrols, spent the rest of the night under it, giving me some respite from the frost.

On the following Saturday morning, my intention had been to go to the Canal Transport offices at Wigan Pier in search of a job, but I decided against it. My reasoning was that I would be asked my name and address and concluded that it wouldn't have been wise to give a local address, and having a Liverpool accent! I changed my plans and decided to make an early start and go to the same company's offices in Pall Mall in Liverpool.

Even under normal circumstances, I imagine it to be a bit of an ordeal for a fourteen year old applying for a first job, there wouldn't have been many like myself, starting out with a *multiple of handicaps*, still being a ward of the courts, and an absconder from a boys' Royal Naval Training Ship.

Now that I was dressed as a working lad, resplendent in my new bib and brace overalls and new cloth cap, I felt sure I must have put two years on my age, and felt more confident of success.

I was certainly feeling relieved at disposing of the bicycle. My hope now was that it would never be discovered that I'd stolen it.

Chapter Ten

Employment

Getting to Liverpool on the Saturday morning proved no problem. Before it was daylight, and after having tea and toast in an early opening market tea room, I was on the Ormskirk Road successfully hitching a lift on a Liverpool bound lorry.

I told the Wigan driver I was looking for a job and he put me off at a spot only a ten minute walk from Pall Mall.

I was not yet 9am as I stood in Tithebarn Street, so I made my way to Exchange railway station for a one penny wash and brush up, before making my way to the canal offices.

Canal Transport Ltd owned and operated about forty motor boats on the Leeds and Liverpool Canal, as well as a few horse drawn, but in 1937 the latter were beginning to be phased out as uneconomical, and oak timbered boats were being replaced by steel constructed ones, all capable of carrying 50 tonnes of non-bulk cargo. This tonnage was restricted however to about 30 tonnes when transporting bales of cotton.

The first barges made of timber were named after the planets, Mars, Mercury, Jupiter, Uranus, Pluto, etc. The iron boats were named mostly after British rivers, the Irwell, Ouse, Humber, Mersey, Clwyd, Ribble, and Tweed, then towards the end of the commercial life of the canal, one iron boat was named after a Liverpool football team, Everton.

Arriving at the main entrance to the office, I tapped on a small sliding window marked *enquiries*. The window was opened by a bespectacled middle aged man, and a little timidly, I asked him if there were any vacancies as a mate on their boats. I was asked to step inside the office, then he closed the window before opening the office door to let me in. I think he wished to keep the warm air in and the cold out.

The man I was speaking to was Mr Ben Wall, a manager and shareholder of the company, he asked me my age and where I lived. I also told him that this was my first application for employment since leaving school two weeks previous. I went on to tell Mr Wall that both my parents and grandparents had worked on the canal, and in fact my father still did.

Family connections

He became a little more interested when I mentioned these facts, I think because the people who normally sought work on the waterway were not Liverpool residents but country folk living alongside the canal, with the largest percentage coming from Burscough Town or thereabouts.

I was asked if my parents knew of my application and were they aware, if I was given a job, it would entail being away from home and sleeping aboard the boat? I gave Mr Wall a positive answer. He went to a corner of the office where he made a telephone call, and then he returned to explain to me that he had been talking to the manager of the Blackburn warehouse; apparently the boat *Jupiter* was tied up there, stranded, because of not having a mate. There had been some trouble between captain and mate resulting in the mate walking off the boat, with no intention of returning.

To me it sounded like a heaven sent opportunity which couldn't have happened at a more opportune time. The captain of the *Jupiter* was a Jack Webster from Burscough Town.

I was informed that the captain was going to be contacted and asked if he would consider taking on board a young learner, fresh from school, and with family connections on the canal? His response was going to be telephoned back from Blackburn in a short while.

While Mr Wall was in the process of asking me more about my family background, to ascertain which part of the closely-knit family of boat people I belonged, because he knew most of them, having been a boatman himself, the telephone rang; it was the manager at Blackburn replying.

He informed Mr Wall that Jack Webster had said he was willing to take me as mate, on a month's trial, to see how I squared up to the job.

I was instructed to start work on the following Monday, two days hence.

Before I left the Pall Mall office I was given a ten shilling note, five shillings was for the train fare to Blackburn, and the other five was an advance in pay.

There was a train leaving Exchange station on the Monday morning at 7 o'clock. to get me to Blackburn before 8am. I assured Mr Wall that I would be on it. As I walked away from Pall Mall I wondered how I was going to spend the weekend until the Monday morning. I did not want to go anywhere near any of my relations, or for them to know I was in Liverpool. I wanted to get established in my new job first, to show every-one it was all I wanted to do.

Making my way up Bevington Hill I passed St Alban's church, the place where my Canadian grandfather had married my Irish grandmother in 1882, fifty six years previous.

I came to Arden House in Bevington Bush, a large Salvation Army Hostel for men, which was a well known and much frequented establish-ment. I went inside and treated myself to a cheap meal of sausage and mashed potatoes, stewed apple and custard, a thick slice of bread, and a mug of tea.

Most of my fellow diners were *gentlemen of the highways and by-ways*, and a good many of them used the canal towpaths, not like myself, as a sanctuary, but because it gave them the feeling of being nearer to nature.

On a notice board, written in chalk, in the dining hall of Arden House, it stated that all bookings for beds had to be paid for by 6pm, with only two consecutive nights stay allowed at any one time, the charge was nine pence per night.

The rule of only allowing a maximum of two nights stay, was to stop anyone living there on a permanent basis, and to keep professional tramps on the move. Any self-respecting *knight of the road* wouldn't want to stay longer anyway.

I booked my bed cubicle for the Saturday and Sunday nights and paid one shilling and sixpence before going for a walk to Paddys Market in Cazenau Street, then returning to Arden House for my tea.

I spent that Saturday evening in the Rotunda Theatre, at the junction of Scotland Road and Kirkdale Road, being entertained by some of the music hall artistes of the time.

I will always remember seing the great Scottish comedian and singer of Scottish songs, Harry Lauder, later Sir Harry, on the *Roundy*, as we Liverpudlians called it. He came onto the stage, walking very slowly, complete with his crooked stick, kilt, and sporran, singing his favourite song: *I Love A Lassie.*

The Rotunda and the Metropole Theatres were both destroyed in the 1940s by German bombs during an air raid.

I finished the evening returning to my ninepenny bed with a handful of chips.

Before I fell asleep in my cubicle that night, fully clothed, I took the advice of another inmate, who must have guessed by my age that I was a *rookie* at sleeping in *Doss Houses* and I tied my boots to the bed to stop them being stolen in the night.

On the following Sunday morning, while having breakfast of bacon and eggs, I decided not to spend a second night in Arden House but instead to start off walking to Blackburn, to save five shillings train fare, and to have an early start in my first job.

I set off walking about 8 o'clock on that cold February morning. I felt the weather for the first half hour, but by the time I had reached Aintree the cold didn't bother me anymore. I was as warm as a piece of toast. Walking through Ormskirk then on to Wigan, I arrived in Blackburn at the canal warehouse at 5pm, after an approximate twenty-two mile walk, on a dry cold sunny day.

There were 4 motor boats tied alongside the wharf, one of which was boat *Jupiter*. There was no sign of life aboard her but on one of the other boats, *Pluto*, a man was busy washing down the decks. He was doing this by skillfully dipping a bucket, tied on a short piece of rope to the handle, into the water, then throwing the water over the decks.

I asked him if he could tell me the whereabouts of Mr Webster. He replied: 'Do's tha mean Jack Webster?' and without waiting for an answer he began shouting: 'Are thee there Jack?' Almost immediately a head popped up in the scuttle hole of the bow cabin of *Jupiter* and shouted back: 'Hello, What's up?' It was captain Jack Webster.

In my formative years at Barnes Home, I had been taught that all adults should be addressed as Mr, Mrs, Madam, Miss, or even Sir. It never occurred to me to call Jack Webster, just Jack.

I was soon to learn that among the working class fraternity, regardless of age or sex, only christian names were used, unless it was an older relative, like Father, Grandparents, Uncles or Aunts.

At Jack's invitation, I descended into the cabin. His first question to me was: 'What's thee name lad, and where dos cum fro?' Giving him all the information he requested, and more details of my family, he asked why I didn't prefer to work with my father? I said I wanted to learn how to work a motor boat, in preference to the horse drawn boats. My explanation seemed reasonable enough to him, he knew my father.

Jack was about thirty years old, and came from a long line of canal

Breaking ice, 1947.

boatmen, and he had started on the canal with his late father, after leaving school. Being one of the younger generation of bargees, he wasn't as old fashioned as some of the others. He was medium build, clean shaven, methodical in his ways, a non-smoker, and teetotal.

He asked me if I'd had my tea or to use his vernacular, what he actually said was: 'Hasta 'ad thee tay lad and dusta like egg and collup?' (bacon). Jack reached for a heavy iron kettle, which was standing on a piece of slate on the cabin's wooden floor, at the side of the stove fire. He proceeded to fill it from a multi-coloured fresh water cask situated *up top*, on the deck, then he placed it on the fire to boil.

Pulling down a hinged lift-up table revealing a shelved cupboard stocked with victuals, he commenced slicing a piece of bacon which had more fat on than lean, and no doubt obtained by barter for some other commodity (part cargo) from one of the scores of canalside farmers.

When the kettle had boiled and the tea mashed, an equally heavy frying pan was produced, into which the bacon was placed, it too was put on the fire.

The rounded tin chimneys on canal boats went up through the deck timbers in slotted sections, to stand approximately three feet above the level of the deck, higher if you wanted on a windy day by adding another 18 inch section, but you had to be mindful of low bridges, and take the top section off again. Because of limited space in a boat's cabin, everything had its own particular storage place, so you knew just where to put your hands on it. Eventually, Jack and myself tucked in to a rib-sticking meal.

He did mention that he wasn't expecting me until the following morning, but I told him I was both eager and excited to make a start, and couldn't wait.

Learning to be a Boatman

When I dropped in on him he was busy making a bow fender, shaping it into a ball, using half inch white cotton rope. Such items were to be seen hanging over the main bow stem timber of most boats, and secured by a chain running through them attached to two metal rings screwed into the deck, one on each side of the stem. Besides being decorative, they also served the practical purpose of protecting the bow in the event of a collision.

On horse drawn boats this white cotton rope was used more extensively. It was seen plaited around the squared top of the wooden rudders, and was known as a stern *Turks Head*, and was purely for decoration. When scrubbed with canal water using a long handled brush it came up snowy white, and made a lovely contrast with the reds, whites, and blues of the paintwork.

The captain of the *Jupiter* and I had a good chinwag before retiring to our respective bunks, one on each side of the cabin. He told me of some of his experiences since he had started on the canal. He was still talking when I fell asleep.

Most boatmen went to bed half dressed, still attired in their long johns, which they wore throughout the day, to keep out the wind. Boating was a very outdoor occupation and pyjamas to them were an unknown garment. It would have been thought of as getting *dressed up* to go to bed.

On the Monday morning Jack was out of his bunk first, when I awoke he had made a plateful of toast, mashed a pot of tea, and a pot of home-made marmalade was on the table. It was probably the smell of the bread toasting that woke me from my slumbers.

When I had finished eating his food, (I was supposed to provide provisions for myself), I was invited to go aft with him, to the engine house, where I was shown the engine itself, how it was started, and how it was maintained throughout the day.

It was a *Widdup* diesel oil engine, and I watched as Jack lit a cartridge with a match, before inserting it into the dome of the cylinder head. While he was waiting for the dome to heat, he filled the gearbox with lubricating oil, and felt the position of the gear lever up top to ascertain it was in the neutral position. After a few minutes he commenced swinging the flywheel backwards and forwards in a semi-circular motion, by gripping the spring loaded, self retracting pull out handle inserted in the flywheel. All at once the whole craft shook and started vibrating in the water as the engine sprung into life, from being a stationary wooden structure the boat had now become a live and noisy object.

We both went back up on deck, where the skipper proceeded to untie the mooring ropes and coil them in neat round piles on the deck. I just stood watching, then Jack told me to go forrid (forward or to the bow) and push the front of the boat away from the canal side using the boat hook (boatmen call it a *shaft*). That was my first act as a performing barge mate. (1938)

I watched more attentively as he took hold of the tiller, and pushed the gear lever into the forward position, causing the fan (propellor) to rotate slowly, pushing the craft ahead, and away from the warehouse quay.

I walked back to the stern end, by way of the 18 inch gunwhale, and sat on the engine house top. When she was in mid-stream the throttle handle was lifted to give the engine more power.

As I sat I took particular note of how the cargo-laden boat was manoeuvred around the twists and turns of the waterway.

It was pointed out to me the importance of steering the boat the furthest way around a bend, more especially when it was loaded and deep in the water, or drawing a bigger draught as boatmen would say. The longest way round is always the deepest, to *cut across* would certainly result in running the boat aground.

One of the most unavoidable occurrences that befalls a motor boat, especially when loaded, and the fan deep in the water, is for the blades to pick up an obstruction; something like a piece of rope or the wire remains of a discarded household bed, criminally thrown into the canal. When such obstacles become entangled around the fan shaft, it can cause hours of delay in attempting to extriate them. It can also cause the engine to jam, necessitating the call out of a fitter from the nearest boat yard. If the offending obstruction cannot be cleared by standing on the stern deck, prodding and pulling at the unseen rubbish with the short shaft, it meant undressing down to your underpants and getting into the water, to try and unravel it by feeling and groping blindly under the water, holding either a pair of wire cutters or a sharp knife in your hands.

We climbed the 7 locks above Blackburn, on through Gannow Tunnel, then Burnley, and tying up at Nelson of all places for the night. It was for me returning to the scene of the crime!

The following day, Tuesday, after reaching Barrowford, climbing all the time, we then started to descend, and finally reached our destination at Skipton.

It was tiring work for me running ahead to turn off the swing bridges and getting the locks ready, but I'd enjoyed every minute of my first two days. I did think to myself once a bicycle would save a lot of boot leather!. I hoped to buy a second-hand one at a later date, all being well.

Besides the work, I also enjoyed meeting lots of other boatmen, young and old, and I think I was about the only one with a Liverpool accent. I felt that not only did I want to look like a bargee, I wanted also to speak like one. After all, it was the way my mother spoke so I was told.

Jack Webster appeared impressed by my agility in running ahead to the locks and bridges, he wasn't aware at this stage of all the practice I'd had over the past three years running from Barnes Home.

He seemed content also at having a keen young learner like myself, rather than one of the older types of mate, sent as replacements. Some were heavy drinkers, and not too clean in their ways and habits, and language. Some liked to live up to the fallacy of being able to *swear like a bargee*, this way of life wouldn't have suited Jack Webster.

It was essential for the good working of the boat, that captain and mate got on well with each other—they had to work and live together in the confined space of a boat's cabin.

Unlike horse drawn boats which had two living cabins bow and stern, motor boats had only one *living in* cabin at the bow, the stern end contained the engine house.

The following morning I helped the captain to remove the large black tarpaulin sheeting covering the large bales of wool, neatly folding them in a special way in order to make it easy to apply them again.

The hold of the boat had always to be kept clean and dry for carrying various foodstuffs such as 4,000 28lb parcels of sugar, in 2lb bags=50 tonnes, or sugar in 1cwt sacks, flour, loose grain, or maybe cartons of sauce were also carried. A lot of the cargoes had to be handled individually and stacked in the hold, and then man-handled out again. It was all good exercise providing your back didn't break.

At 7.30 the warehouse men arrived, and started to use a hand winched lifting crane which was fitted with grappling irons at the end of chains to grab out the cotton bales. In less than two hours the job was completed with some of the overdue bales being put straight onto a horse drawn cart then pulled direct to the spinning mill.

As a consequence the boat was now *light* or empty and it was the first time I'd seen her so high in the water. She would be able to travel faster now due to the engine not having to shove 25 tonnes of wool along. *Jupiter's* carrying capacity was fifty-five tonnes providing it was not a bulk cargo such as wool or machinery.

Horse drawn boats were six to seven feet longer than a motor boat, and could carry up to seventy tonnes, but only on the Leeds and Liverpool canal, and only between Liverpool and Wigan. The reason was that the locks beyond Wigan are not long enough to accommodate the 70-foot long boats.

This canal carried far more tonnage than all the other inland barge canals in Britain.

The other type of canal boat on other canals known as *narrow boats* which had a carrying capacity of only twenty-five tonnes total did not ply the Leeds and Liverpool.

After discharging the cargo, Jack Webster went to the company office for further instructions. He returned to say the orders were to proceed *down cut* to Wigan warehouse and load machinery for the Liverpool warehouse.

Stocking up

Before we set sail, Jack and I went to some shops close by to buy provisions such as tea, condensed tinned milk, bread, and margarine. Other food, such as eggs, bacon, and cheese, etc., were bought direct from the farms adjacent to the canal where they could be obtained fresher and cheaper. It was well on into the morning when we left Skipton bound for Wigan.

When we'd travelled a short distance I was invited by the captain to take hold of her, meaning to man the tiller, and steer the boat. He had given me plenty of verbal tuition, and now some practical experience. Jack sat on the engine house top, watching and guiding me, and commanding me to slow her down when approaching the narrow bridge holes. (He didn't want me to knock any of them down).

There are only three basic commands given to someone at the tiller when navigating a boat along this inland waterway (I don't know about other canals). These instructions are: *Hold In, Hold Out,* and *Hard Over Hold In* means to push the tiller towards the towpath to the right (Starboard). *Hold Out* is to push it away from the towpath to the left (Port) *Hard Over* means to push the tiller as far as it will go, either Port or Starboard, and as quickly as possible, perhaps to avoid a collision.

The bow responds by turning in the opposite direction to the way the tiller is moved. At times the towpath is on your left facing forward, or is on the right.

There are a number of *change over bridges* on the route, which entails walking the horses across the bridges, when the path ends on one side and continues on the opposite side, past the bridge. The towing mast has also to be changed over, to the same side as the path.

We made it to back to Blackburn that Wednesday night, my tenth night of being A.W.O.L. from Blyth, setting a kind of record for myself. My previous time for being absent from Barnes Home was nine days and nights.

We tied up, had our tea, then spent some time in the stables, talking to other boatmen until Jack reminded me that we had a hard day ahead of us, working *Jupiter* down the twenty-one Wigan Locks, before tying up at the Wigan warehouse, so we retired to our bunks soon after 10pm.

By the time we reached the bottom of Wigan Locks in the late afternoon of Thursday, I realized what the captain meant when he said it was a hard slog negotiating them, especially when you have had a *bad road* down, on account of the volume of traffic.

Jack's knowledge of the location of the fish and chip shops along the 127-mile length of the cutting was second to none. When the boat was safely tied up in Wigan Basin, I was dispatched to a chippy in Wallgate just a few minutes walk away.

While I waited my turn to be served among the clog clad customers, mostly women and girls wearing shawls, Barnes Home and The Wellesley Nautical School seemed a world away and an eternity ago. I suddenly thought of the possibility of all this coming to an end, and being taken away from this happy environment and back to the conditions of misery and incarceration. Momentarily such thoughts made me feel sad, then it was my turn to be served.

As soon as I spoke, asking for a fish and two pennyworth twice, the local customers waiting knew there was a stranger in the shop on account of my different dialect. I, on the other hand, didn't feel like a stranger, I felt as though I belonged amongst them.

Because of my willingness to learn, and do as I was told, I think Jack Webster was quite happy to carry out the extra work my inexperience caused him. For instance, he had to spend longer hours at the tiller than he would normally, if he'd had a more proficient mate, and he had always to keep a wary eye on my activities and performance, especially at the locks, to see and avoid getting into any trouble, or putting the boat into any danger.

Whilst I was steering the boat and still learning he also had to be attentive, whereas with an experienced mate he would have been able to relax in the bow cabin. He had also to sit on the engine house eating his meals guiding me, and making sure I didn't stave in any bow planks, by colliding and possibly scuttling the craft.

It was still early evening when we finished the fish and chips, and I was asked if I would like to go to a local picture house to pass a couple of hours away instead of sitting in the cabin all evening. Sensing I might not have enough money, Jack quickly added that it would be *his treat*.

Making sure the engine house and the cabin were locked, we started to walk the dimly lit streets, until we came to a small cinema in a side street, just off Wallgate. It was advertising as the main feature one of the many Tarzan films hat were all the rage about that time. I remember it was very warm and stuffy in this small building. After the hard day I'd had, pushing and shoving lock gates, I fell asleep as it was being shown. It was past 10pm when we made our way back to the boat.

In the 1930s, people were inclined to retire to their beds earlier than they do today. One reason was that most commenced work at 7am in the factories and mills. As we walked down Wallgate, I wondered if Jack would be disturbing some of them with the clatter of his clogs on the pavement? I was wearing Naval issue boots which hardly made a sound.

Unlike 99% of all boatmen, I never wore clogs, I preferred bouncy rubber.

When we reached the wooden double gates of the Canal Transport Wharf which had been closed for the night, we gained entry through the small wicket gate. The yard was lit by a solitary gas lamp which burned throughout the night. It was meant as a guide and a precaution to stop boatmen who had had too much to drink, from walking into the canal and being drowned. It had happened more than once on different parts of the route.

Arrested yet again

As we entered the yard, I saw two men silhouetted against the lamp both were wearing trilby hats, my heart started to beat quicker as soon as I saw them. I guessed who they were and what they wanted. For a few seconds I froze with fright, not able to make up my mind whether to turn about and make a dash back through the wicket gate, or hope I was wrong in my assumptions.

As Jack and I got closer to them one of the men spoke to Jack asking: 'Are you Mr Jack Webster?' to which he replied: 'That's me.' The same man then asked: 'Is this your mate Robert Houghton?' Before Jack had time to answer, I made a sudden retreat towards the gate but to no avail. The second man had anticipated such a move, and in a flash he had hold of me in a firm grip. He then produced a pair of handcuffs, and locked them on my small wrists.

One of the men, who seemed to be the senior of the two, then introduced himself as a detective sergeant from Wigan Police Head-quarters and told me I was being arrested and taken to the station for being an absconder from a Naval Training Ship. Captain Jack just stood dumbfounded in disbelief and said nothing.

As I was escorted through the gate, I couldn't bring myself to look back at Jack and say: 'Goodbye'. I felt after all his kindness to me I had let him down.

All the way to the police station I sobbed my heart out and couldn't bear to think of being taken two hundred miles back to Newcastle. For the first time, I wished it had only been to Heaton Mersey twenty miles away.

If anyone had ever asked me, only a couple of weeks previous, would I ever miss Barnes Home, my answer would have been an emphatic 'Never'. I now found myself thinking of all the friendly faces of the boys there, faces I had been banished from ever seeing again. I thought of Louis Gladwin from Halifax, my best pal John Marshall from Wallsend, George Marshall from Oldbury, Sydney Plowright from Nottingham, John Copeland from Waterloo, and many more.

This experience taught me at a very early age that you don't always appreciate and value what you've got until you lose it.

When we arrived at the main bridewell at Wigan the large wooden framed clock on the wall said it was just turned 11pm. With very little formality I was locked in a cell and the door banged shut and locked.

I hardly slept that night but lay on the wooden mattress thinking a thousand different things, here I was in another police cell, when only a few short hours ago, I was in the outside world working and earning my living and feeling happy at doing so, although, always at the back of my mind, since being on the run, I knew authority would eventually catch up with me.

I began to notice that people were beginning to treat me more as a youth than a schoolboy. It must have been the overalls and the cloth cap, and I began to ponder what was to become of me.

This latest nightmare of forcing me to train for the eventual enlistment into the Royal Navy was something I could not possibly cope with.

I knew I would never stop running no matter what the punishment. It was being able to run that kept giving me the spirit to fight back so to speak.

The following morning I was given breakfast, later taken to the lavatory and then to wash my hands and face.

The next person to visit me was the detective sergeant who apprehended me at the boat warehouse. He greeted me with: 'Hello Robert, did you sleep well?' I was always being asked silly questions, part of the diplomacy I suppose. He sat down beside me, with a note pad resting on his knees and a fountain pen in his hand. On seeing the tray with the empty plate and mug on it, he remarked: 'You've had your breakfast then', I replied: 'Yes Thank you'.

He questioned me about my activities over the past ten days since leaving Blyth. The first question he put to me was: 'Where did you get the civilian clothes from and where is the Naval Uniform?' I replied by saying I'd bought the working clothes in Paddys Market in Liverpool with money given to me as an advance in wages by Canal Transport and how I'd saved the train fare also given to me, by walking to Blackburn to join the boat.

I was still wearing the short-legged trousers under the long-legged overalls and the jacket which was the suit taken from the Barnes Home. I also had with me the blue gaberdine raincoat.

Quite abruptly, the detective said: 'You broke into Barnes Home last Thursday didn't you?'. As I was wearing the incriminating evidence, it was pointless to deny the fact. I guessed he also knew I discarded the uniform there. Realizing he already knew the answers to questions he was putting to me I was resigned to telling him the truth, but not all of it.

He did not know about the bicycle I'd stolen in Nelson, and the selling of it in Wigan Market, and I never mentioned it to him. In fact, I have never ever told anyone about it until now!.

The policeman was putting the questions to me in an affable manner, and I did not want to annoy him by telling him obvious lies. I wanted him to remain friendly, because at that moment I needed to hear a non-hostile voice as I was feeling so utterly dejected and lonely.

My thoughts were to the future which looked so bleak and hopeless just then. I was asked how I got to Heaton Mersey from Blyth and eventually to Liverpool, how had I lived and where did I sleep at night, etc.

When Mr Rose, the detective, was convinced that I wasn't responsible for the countless crimes committed in the last ten days in Northumberland, Durham, all of Yorkshire and Lancashire, he prepared to leave. Putting a few sweets in my hand he informed me I would be appearing before the magistrates in the juvenile court that morning.

I was to see Mr Rose once more, when he gave evidence in the court, describing how I was arrested, *as a result of information received*, and how I had been given employment as a barge mate, by pretending I was a recent school leaver when in fact I was a ward of the court and an absconder from The Wellesley Nautical School.

Back to Newcastle

A remand in custody was requested, and granted, to await an escort to take me back to Newcastle-Upon-Tyne, to face charges of defrauding the L.N.E.R. and for *further investigations'.*

About noon that same day, another plain clothes policeman came to my cell. He said his name was Mr Barrow (another sergeant) and he was going to escort me to Newcastle. He expressed the hope that I would was not cause him any trouble in the process by trying to escape during the journey. With that he left the cell, saying we would be starting out after dinner time, (lunch). He returned an hour later and instructed me to put on the gaberdine raincoat, then he handcuffed my wrist to his remarking: 'If you behave yourself these will come off when we've boarded the train'.

We left the bridewell in a car for a five-minute drive to the Wigan North Western Station, where we boarded a train for Manchester, there we changed onto another for Newcastle.

En route to changing trains, Mr Barrow bought himself a newspaper from a bookstall and he also purchased a boys' book for me to read.

Although some effort was made to conceal the handcuffs from the public, they were noticed by some of the more observant, or nosey parkers, and we became objects of curiosity to a few by their quick glances, to me especially, as the prisoner, and at my apparent tender age, despite my still wearing working Wigan Market overalls.

The train for Newcastle was already standing on the platform when we arrived. We entered a carriage and sat in an empty compartment of the corridor train. The handcuffs were removed, and I was told to take off my raincoat before settling in a corner of the compartment. Mr Barrow sat opposite reading his newspaper.

I tried to get absorbed in the book he had given me, but my thoughts were elsewhere.

Before the train departed, a man and a woman entered the compartment and sometime later, when the train was on its way, the policeman got into conversation with our fellow travellers. During their talk I heard the name of Adolf Hitler mentioned and the possibility of an impending war with Germany. They spoke of our Prime Minister, Neville Chamberlain, and a certain Mrs Simpson, who was to marry ex-King Edward the Eighth.

I was much too busy thinking my own thoughts about my own troubles.

I thought of my first workmate, Jack Webster, and how he would be stranded once again, this time at Wigan, awaiting the arrival of yet another mate, before he could continue working the boat *Jupiter*.

One bright but short-lived respite from my abject misery, as the train sped further north away from my native Bootle, was when the policeman took me along the corridor to the dining car for afternoon tea.

I had never experienced such luxurious surroundings before, the carpeted floor, spotless white tablecloths, a small lamp on each table, and a white coated waiter to serve us.

It was dark when the train pulled into Newcastle Station. The journey had been long and slow; Mr Barrow said our arrival was an hour overdue, although I was in no hurry to meet what I expected to be my impending doom.

Chapter Eleven

My Fate awaits me

We were met on the station platform by a uniformed police officer. He was the driver of a car parked outside the station entrance, which caused a few more eyes to be cast in our direction.

We were taken to the police headquarters where I was once more deposited in a cell for the night. My thoughts then were of a condemned man knowing the time for his execution was drawing nearer.

Ever since being put into Barnes Home I'd become an avid clock watcher, before then, time had never held any great significance for me, excepting at 4pm on schooldays, when it was time to go home and do my own things.

After spending another sleepless night on the boards of a cell, the door was opened and in came *room service* with my breakfast.

An hour later I was being grilled again, this time by the Newcastle C.I.D. and on the same pattern as that used in other *nicks*. They were trying to find a culprit to fit an abundance of unsolved crimes, and I was questioned to see if I could assist in clearing up a few of them. All their enquiries received a negative response from me.

Later I was taken to a room similar to the one I knew at Bootle Town Hall. It contained a very long table with many chairs on each side on which men and women were already seated. The room bore no resemblance to a court of law.

At the top of the table sat a fairly elderly, refined, and stern looking lady. She looked elderly to me, being just turned fourteen. In reality she was probably in her fifties. This lady was in charge of the proceedings.

I was ordered to position myself at the opposite end of the table, facing her. I stood standing to attention scarcely daring to breath. One of the men stood up and started to speak addressing his words to the lady he called *Your Worship*, (up until then, I had only been taught to worship God). He commenced by giving an abbreviated history of me from the time I was sent to Barnes Home and of my family background at the time, then right up to the present.

He continued by relating how I had absconded from The Wellesley Nautical School, after being there only a matter of hours, and he mentioned the burglary at Barnes Home, and finally of being apprehended at Wigan.

When he had finished speaking, there was a general discussion between themselves held in lowered tones after which *Your Worship* addressed me personally to ask: 'Why do you keep runing away?' I replied simply and briefly: 'I want to go home'. She then asked: 'Don't you want to go into the Royal Navy when you're old enough?' I replied: 'No Miss'. Whether I was addressing her in the correct manner I knew not, I was endeavouring to be as polite as I knew how, surmising that this lady had the power of life and death over me.

Return to the cells

At the end of more whispered conversation, her Worship announced the verdict of the court. Again directing her words to me, she said: 'The Captain of The Wellesley Nautical School has informed the court that he does not want you back in his school so you are to be remanded in custody for two weeks for further reports'. With those last words the proceedings came to an end. I was beckoned by a plain clothes policeman to accompany him out of the room, and back to my own private cell.

Some hours later the cell door was opened, and I found my self rather hurriedly being handcuffed to another male. He was a lot taller and much older than I, but like me, he was a prisoner. We were ushered to the end of the corridor to an open gate, backed up to which was a dark painted van; It was a Black Maria. It already contained more prisoners, handcuffed to what I first thought were police officers, until I read the three large capital letters H.M.P. on their shoulder lapels.

The last time I saw those letters was when I called at houses near to Walton Prison, near my home in Bootle, in Walton, Liverpool. I was selling home-made bundles of firewood at the time and the man who answered the door and bought three one-penny bundles from me (I never forgot such addresses) wore similar lapels. I now knew I wa. being remanded to prison for the next two weeks!

Until that moment, I'd always been of the opinion that I was too young to qualify for an adult prison, where they hung people by the neck until they were dead, apparently I was mistaken.

Eventually the Black Maria arrived at its destination, Durham Prison. The vehicle had been let into the jail through two sets of double gates then the rear doors of the van were opened to reveal to us the prison yard. We all clambered out and onto the concrete yard when the hand cuffs were removed.

Immediately I was instructed by a warder to accompany him in a different direction to that taken by the other prisoners. This warder, unlike the others, wore a white starched jacket with a red cross on both arms denoting he was a medical orderly.

After the ritual of unlocking and locking doors and gates and climbing stairs, we entered the hospital wing of the prison, and into one of the wards, where I was to spend the next two weeks.

I was taken to a bathroom and ordered to remove all my clothes and step into a warm bath prepared by one of the elderly inmates.

When I'd finished bathing I was handed the blue prison issue dressing gown to put on being observed all the time by a medical orderly. I was then shown to a corner bed in the ward and told to get in it.

I thought at the time, the intention was to keep me in bed naked for the next two weeks, to make sure I didn't escape from the institution in view of the reputation I had deservedly acquired, of being an habitual absconder.

It would have been an embarrassment to them I suppose, if a fourteen year old who could climb walls lke a monkey, was to escape.

As things turned out, my assumptions were unfounded by the arrival of the prison doctor, who gave me a thorough examination behind screens placed around my bed.

Later I was measured up by another prisoner for the prison uniform. Apparently it was this prisoner's regular detail to perform this duty on new arrivals, he could have been an *ex-Burtons salesman* gone wrong because the trousers I was eventually given, were four or five inches too long in the leg, and had to be rolled up, likewise the jacket, in the arms. The neck of the shirt collar was inches too big, in fact I wouldn't have looked out of place as a clown in a travelling circus. Not that it mattered because I wasn't due to make any more personal appearances for the next two weeks.

In the prisons of 1938 you had to ask permission to speak to a warder, and when you did, you had to call him *Sir*, and it was one prisoner to each cell. To have a book from the prison library, or to use tobacco was a special privilege not granted immediately on admission. Contact with the outside world was very restricted. There was definitely no wirelesses or newspapers in the cells, and television was not yet available to anybody.

Not that I'm an authority on prisons, never having been in one since 1938, but from what I read there is not the same discipline in them as there used to be.

What I now know is that although transportation to the colonies had long been abolished for adult convicted felons, it was not the case as regards children who were wards of court or in orphanages or other children's institutions up and down the country.

Up to as late as the 1940, children were being transported to places like Australia, without them having any say in the matter, to work as domestics, or on farms, or both. Rumour had it that some boys were sent from Barnes Home which I feel could well be true. But for me having brothers and sisters it could have happened to me, and it's a long walk from Australia!

My two weeks in Durham Jail (without a number) seems more like a funny episode to me now. It did keep me safe, and made sure that I put in an appearance at the appointed time at Newcastle Juvenile Court.

My stay was not unpleasant, and, as things turned out, I wouldn't have missed the eventful appearance for the world.

Whilst in the hospital wing, every morning when breakfast was over, which I had helped to distribute and collect the empty pots, I was given the job of pulling and pushing a long handled *dummy* over the highly polished and already slippery floor.

In the evenings, after tea time, when most of the chores were completed, I always had a library book chosen for me to read by the side of my bed. During my stay I just about earned my board and keep, by today's union rates of pay I would have been owed something. At 8pm every night, I was ordered to get into bed.

A coincidence

To speak of another incident during my remand in jail, I have first to go back to the winter evenings of 1936 when I was in Barnes Home. During those times I started to attend St John Ambulance classes, First Aid being taught one evening every week.

A St John Ambulance man named Mr Chapman was our instructor. He visited the Home to teach classes the rudiments of first aid, ie, how to apply a splint to a fractured bone, etc. At the end of the winter sessions, and after a short verbal and practical examination, we were awarded a certificate of competence.

One morning whilst out exercising, by walking a circular path on a small garden in front of the hospital buildings, with a white-coated warder looking on and occasionally glancing at his watch, I went to pass in front of him, he beckoned me to stop and stand by his side, by calling my surname. He said: 'Weren't you once in Barnes Home at Heaton Mersey," and I replied: 'Yes Sir'. Then he turned his head to look down at me from under the grenadier-type peaked cap and his six feet plus height and continued: 'You were in the first aid classes there?' again I answered: 'Yes Sir.' He then asked: 'Don't you remember me? I was your instructor.' Taking a closer look at his face I recognized Mr Chapman.

He did not add any more to the conversation only to tell me to rejoin the *walking wounded* prisoners in single file on the path, each one with his own thoughts.

It was during my second week in the prison, Mr Chapman commenced a duty of 6pm to 6am (I don't think they work such long hours today). At about 7pm on the Monday when all the chores on the ward had been completed and things were quiet, I was sitting in the chair by my bed trying to get interested in a library book, but my thoughts were distracted by thinking of the future.

Mr Chapman, now the night orderly, was seated behind a table, at the side of the locked gate. He called me over and to my surprise, asked me if I knew how to play draughts (chequers). I replied: 'No Sir. I was invited to pull up a chair, and he started to teach me the rules of the game for about an hour, after which I was instructed to return to my bed to get some sleep.

I was given this tuition every evening of that week. Mr Chapman was smart at playing the game and, to this day, I have never forgotten the moves he taught me, nor have I forgotten the man himself.

Although he never spoke of or mentioned my troubles while we were playing the game, he gave me the feeling that he was on my side, and was like a father figure to me. He made my stay in Durham Jail much less miserable and less lengthy, I don't think he looked on me as just another prisoner, but as a young boy he could teach something useful to.

On the night he knew would be my last for our pleasant little get togethers, Mr Chapman wished me luck, and suggested I write to him if I wished, care of the prison, to let him know what was happening to me. I very much regret to say I never did contact him after I left the prison.

I guessed he was born in Newcastle or thereabouts because he spoke with a Geordie accent. In 1938 he must have been in his fifties, so today he will no doubt be pushing up daisies somewhere and, if so, no doubt they will be large good hearted ones like the man himself.

On the Monday morning I was due to appear before the magistrates at Newcastle, I was awakened at 6am. The clothes I'd been wearing when I arrived had been brought to my bedside, and had been washed and pressed. My socks, which had holes in them when they were taken from me, had been darned, and my well worn boots, which must have covered over a hundred miles since they were given to me brand new at The Wellesley Nautical School, were repaired and polished. The same quality of service could not have been bettered in a five-star hotel!

One item missing was the long-legged overalls which I'd part exchanged in Wigan Market for the stolen bicycle. I was to be taken back to Newcastle, along with other prisoners, in the Black Maria, dressed as a short-trousered schoolboy once more. It was turned 7am when we left the prison.

As I climbed into the van, handcuffed once more to another prisoner, my short trousers were the object of some subdued amusement. I overheard one of the accompanying warders remark to a colleague: 'This place is beginning to look more like a kindergarten every day'.

It was a bitter cold March morning as we proceeded to the Newcastle courts. We sat on both sides of the vehicle, both warders and prisoners facing each other. We were rocked and jostled as the van unexpectedly manoeuvred corners we were unable to anticipate.

On arrival at the court buildings I was again singled out from the adults and led upstairs into the same room from where I'd been remanded a fortnight before.

We sat and waited for the senior members of the judiciary to arrive, I being kept under close surveillance. As the minutes ticked by, I felt myself beginning to shake with fear, thinking of the impending ordeal, and imagining I could hear the stern looking woman, who had remanded me to prison, pronouncing some unbearable sentence on me.

Pronunciation of Sentence

Suddenly, all those present in the court were ordered to *be upstanding*, as the lady magistrate came into the room, and took her seat at the head of the table. To my horror, she looked straight at me, as she sat down at the opposite end to where I was standing.

Her first words were addressed to me directly and, all at once, they transformed the atmosphere from one of strict disciplinarianism to one of warm caring. She said, gesticulating with her arm: 'Come here Robert', inviting me to walk the length of the long table and stand beside her. I had almost gone numb with fear before she entered the room and I was having difficulty getting my legs to function. My feelings were like Oliver Twist, when he was about to ask for more!

When I arrived at her side, this strong faced lady actually put her arms around my waist and started talking to me. She said: 'I've been told that when you were apprehended at Wigan in Lancashire you were being employed as a barge mate on the canal.' By now, speech had almost deserted me also, but I managed to nod my head and reply: 'Yes Miss.'

The magistrate went on to explain to me, that during the past two weeks whilst I was being held in jail, the court had been making enquiries. She digressed momentarily to say: 'You don't want to spend the rest of your life in places like that do you?' Then she continued: 'We only sent you there for your own protection and safety and not as a punishment.'

What she revealed to me next made my heart beat a little faster, not with fear or despondency, but with great excitement and expectancy.

The court, she said, had received a letter from Mrs Ann Bowen and her daughter Mrs Margaret Spencer, both of Lock Cottages, Appley Bridge, Wigan. In their joint letter she said they had pleaded to the court to release me into their custody and care.

Since receiving the letter an officer of the court had made the long journey south to Appley Lock to visit the cottages and interview them both. Jack Spencer, the son-in-law and special constable, had said he was willing to keep an eye on me also along with his own three sons.

When the chairperson of the court made her final remarks to tell me it had been decided to release me into the care of Mrs Bowen I knew a dream had come true.

After the verdict, the stern looking chairman of the court said, in an unemotional and almost impatient manner: 'Now go along with Mr Chandler to probation officer and don't let us see you before this court again.' From that moment I was free; It had seemed a long time since I'd been taken off the streets of Bootle and sent to Heaton Mersey.

The charges of defrauding the L.N.E.R. and breaking into Barnes Home were not proceeded with but adjourned Sine-Die.

I've often thought since what might have been the outcome of it all had the court known of the stolen bicycle.

Chapter Twelve

Final release and freedom

From Newcastle Juvenile Court I was taken to the Probation Room and given tea and sandwiches, then I was taken around the city to a boys' outfitters. A new long-trousered suit, two shirts, two sets of underclothes, socks, one pair of shoes, a pullover, raincoat, and a small attache case, were bought for me by the Probation Officer.

In the different shops we went into Mr Chandler produced a document of identity and authorization and simply signed for the articles purchased. I do not know where the bills were sent, perhaps it was a government department?

The suit and the raincoat I was wearing at the time, taken from Barnes Home, were taken from me, and no doubt returned there.

I was never to know headmaster J. H. Rowe's reaction when he was informed, as I'm sure he was, that I had been released into the custody of Mrs Bowen. A request and a decision refused only a short time ago by the governing body of Barnes Home.

It has crossed my mind that perhaps they received some kind of commission for finding recruits, willing or unwilling, for the armed forces, or for transportation to the colonies.

At 3.30pm on the day of my final court appearance, March 1938, Mr Chandler and myself boarded a train at Newcastle Station for the journey south to Manchester and then on to Wigan. It was 10pm when the train pulled into Wallgate Station.

Mrs Bowen had been informed of our arrival time, and was expected to meet us at the station. Sure enough, as I stepped off the train and onto the platform I immediately made out the figure of her and her son-in-law standing and waiting and, as usual, never letting me down.

She was wearing an ankle length dress and coat and her bonnet was tied on her head by a ribbon under her chin boatwoman style.

We all four went into a waiting room where Mrs Bowen, my appointed guardian, was asked to sign papers presented to her by the probation officer. He was not to accompany me any further but, as he told us, he would be staying overnight at a Wigan Hotel, returning to Newcastle the following morning. Mr Chandler shook hands with all three of us, and reminded me to appreciate all that had been done on my behalf by all concerned. With that he was gone, his mission completed.

We caught the last Southport stopping train to Appley Bridge and walked from the station, via the canal towpath, to the Lock Cottages.

I arrived for the first time, with no fear of being picked up and taken elsewhere by the boys in blue.

I was given the back bedroom as my own at 2 Lock Cottages and from the small window I could look up the hills and see Ashurst Beacon.

The brickworks

A bit further along the canal bank, at the front of the cottages, could be seen Parbold Hill. The cottages and the canal lay in a wide valley.

During that week Mrs Bowen took me to Wigan Market to buy me some heavy working boots and overalls in preparation to start work at the brick works at Appley Bridge the following Monday.

While we were in the market I saw the stall-holder with whom I bartered the stolen bicycle only a matter of a few weeks previous; thankfully we did not approach his stall, what I required was bought elsewhere.

Mrs Bowen's three grandchildren, the Spencer boys who lived next door, were all a bit younger than myself and still going to school at Appley Bridge. Horace was the eldest at twelve then came Eric and Cecil.

Their father, besides being a special constable, still worked at the linoleum works at Appley Bridge. His wife Maggie was kept busy looking after the four of them.

I was very happy living at the cottages enjoying the boys company and going with them on Saturdays to visit the shops in Wigan, or sometimes to the pictures for a couple of hours then ride home on the Southport Stopper.

While I was at the brick works I used to see my father working his horse drawn boat, he had a grey haired old man with him as his mate.

The yard of the brick works backed right up to the canal side, and I saw him as he passed by, he would either be going in the direction of Wigan, with an empty boat, or loaded with a cargo of coal for Liverpool. There was just time to shout a few words of greeting, and to have a short conversation with him. Over the past few years he had become a half stranger to me.

My job at the brick works, where I started at 7.30am until 5.30pm on weekdays and 7.30 until 12 noon Saturday mornings, was to store the warm bricks in the yard to cool, not a very exciting occupation. My wages were twelve shillings and sixpence a week, (62½p) of which I gave Mrs Bowen nine shillings to help feed and clothe me.

After working there for six months I began to get restless, there wasn't much of a future in what I was doing and to be a bargee was in my blood. I wanted to continue where I was abruptly stopped, when working with Jack Webster, on the modern form of canal transport, diesel-driven boats.

I had realized right from the start that there was an obstacle to my being able to travel and be away from home. Part of the conditions of my release was that I should at all times reside at 2 Lock Cottages until I was sixteen. Regardless of this, Mrs Bowen, knowing I was getting fed up working at the brick works, said she would ask around by telephoning boat owners in Liverpool. Within three weeks she got me a job with Richard Williams & Sons of 24 Chapel Street, Liverpool, the company she acted as agent for, and the one my father worked for.

I was to join the motor boat *Progress* moored at Haskayne Bridge near Ormskirk. The captain was a Jem Webster, one of the many inter-related, and non-related Websters on the canal.

The captain lived in a canal side cottage close to the bridge, and right opposite the Ship Inn pub, which is 10 miles *down cut* from Appley Lock, towards Liverpool.

One Monday morning in September 1938, Mrs Bowen saw me off hitching a ride on the boat *Venus*, Captain Jemmy Lawson (otherwise known as Ripo).

Jem Webster

I was carrying a wicker basket laden with food, eating utensils and clean underwear.

It took the boat *Venus*, unladen as she was, just over an hour to reach Haskayne Bridge. As we came alongside the *Progress*, I hopped from one boat to the other clutching the basket. Jem Webster came out of his cottage to greet me with the much used bargee expression of 'Hello Little Mate' and inviting me to put my basket in the bow cabin.

By now it was 11 o'clock, and within minutes of my arrival, the captain went below into the engine house to prepare to set sail for Liverpool.

The *Progress* was loaded with 48 tonnes of coal for Tate and Lyle's sugar refinery. From Haskayne it was a six to seven hour journey into the heart of Liverpool depending on the elements.

Jem Webster was a man in his late fifties, and from what I'd been told about him by Tom and Ann Bowen, he was a steady non-drinking man, inclined to be a bit on the miserable side, and very careful with his money.

He lived in the cottage with his wife, who did not enjoy good health, and he had a daughter in her early twenties.

We were soon under way, with the captain steering, and me sitting on the engine house top, ready to jump off to turn the wooden swing bridges. I soon found that Jem Webster wasn't a very talkative man.

As we were sailing along, I made a few brief references to my pedigree, and mentioned my father *Dick Ranty*. I think he already knew who I was.

If you compared my father to Jem Webster, they were completely different in every way. For all his faults, my dad was happy-go-lucky, and certainly not mean, on the contrary, he was a fool with his money. Another difference was that Jem Webster could read and write a little.

I'd been the mate aboard the *Progress* for twelve months when the Prime Minister Mr Neville Chamberlain declared war on Germany. I had got to know Jem Webster very well, he was indeed a miserable kind of man, with no sense of humour whatsoever, and very mean: this extended to habits like smoking used tea leaves in his pipe, and breaking hard mouldy bread into mugs of tea rather than throw it away. Occasionally he would treat himself to a half ounce of pipe tobacco.

What I disliked most of all, and secretly objected to, was the manner in which the boat was operated which, I'd been informed, was the reason why the last mate left.

It was the captain's perogative in deciding the time we started off in the mornings, how far we travelled, and the time we ceased work for the day, and tied up for the night.

It was habit of Jem Webster that, whenever we arrived at the Ship Inn, and his cottage, perhaps even in the middle of the afternoon, he would tie up for the night, and retire to the more comfortable amenities of the cottage until the following morning, while I was left to twiddle my thumbs in the confined space of the cabin, miles from any form of entertainment or pastime.

I was never invited in to share a little of the comfort of his cottage.

To make up for the time lost, I would then be awakened at about 4am, sometimes it would still be dark, frosty and wet, and proceed to wherever we were going.

In contrast, we would pass places of habitation, like Burscough Town, on our way to Liverpool, when it was way past tying up time, and we would continue on for another hour or so, to again finish up at Haskayne, with a late start the following morning. This routine did not suit me at all.

I was still too young to frequent pubs nor had I a desire to do so. At *th' Institute* at Burscough Bridge, or *Bosca*, as we called it, films were shown on most week nights and Saturdays and I loved going to the pictures whenever I got the opportunity.

The captain of the *Progress* had reached the age when he was not interested in making more money, like some of the other boats, by completing five trips a fortnight, carrying five cargoes to Liverpool. Instead he was content to do only four, and that too did not suit my younger and more ambitious aspirations.

I had mentioned some of these facts to both my dad and Tom and Ann Bowen. They all agreed it wasn't right, to be getting me out of my bunk at four in the morning. Mrs Bowen said she would have a word with the owner of the company, Mr Arnold Jones, at the offices in Chapel Street, Liverpool. I should have left the matter in her hands, and awaited the result, but being an impetuous sixteen year old, I decided on a course of action of my own. It was an act probably never perpetrated by a canal boat mate before or since, and its execution was to earn me the life lasting nickname of *Bucko* among the boating fraternity. The name was an abbreviation for buccaneer.

Mutiny on the 'Progress'

One morning in November at about 1am, after being moored at the Ship Inn since 3pm that afternoon, unladen, and en route for Wigan, I rose from my bunk, dressed, jumped down onto the bank, and loosened *Progress* from her berth and shoved her over to the towpath side. I then proceeded to bow haul (pull) her along a two bridge length to Halsall Bridge which took me half an hour. I clambered down into the engine house and started the engine. When it roared into life the noise must have awakened the rural community of farmers and their labourers, after the still quiet of the night was shattered.

Ten minutes after getting under way I passed alongside Scarisbrick Wood, then I came to New Lane wooden swing bridge, I navigated through this by putting the boat to the side, running ahead to swing it off, running back, and steering the boat through, then back again, to put it on again. To have left the bridge off could have caused a vehicle, or any thing else, to have run straight into the water, especially on a dark morning such as this one was.

At 3am I was entering the first lock from Liverpool, Appley Lock. It was ready for climbing when I got to it, at the Liverpool level, so I sailed straight in. To close the gates behind the boat, I had to climb the slippery metal ladder, built into the rock wall (the deepest lock of the ninety-one on the 127-mile length).

The routine then was to wind up the paddles at the other set of gates, to open the sluices, and bring the boat up to the next level, and on course for Wigan.

During the operations, I kept glancing at the cottages below, which were in total darkness, with the Bowens in bed unaware of the bit of drama that was going on outside.

I was trying to imagine the expression on Jem Webster's face when he came out of his cottage at about 4am, to find to his command was not at its moorings.

Then I began to think of the possible consequences of my escapade. I would probably be *drummed out of the service*, or just given the sack. But I'd done the act and there was no turning back. I was now committed to go and load the coal and keep the boat safe from damage.

The locks at Wigan, especially the two at Poolstock, were always frequented by plenty of willing hands ready to help you in negotiating them. In return you allowed them to pillage a small amount of the cargo, perhaps only a bucketful, about four pennyworth at current prices, to warm their homes, and maybe a house full of children.

When one or two of these helpers realized that I was working the boat single handed, they became like busy bees around a jam pot. I knew more than they about navigating and what needed to be done, so I had to assert a little bit of authority, as *acting captain*, by allowing just two of

Steam-driven wide boat carrying coal to Manchester on the 'Leigh Cut'.

the *coal touts* to accompany me across Wigan Ince Moss, to Garswood Hall loading cradle, to help load the cargo.

Ince Moss is on the Leigh Branch of the Leeds and Liverpool Canal, it leads to the Bridgewater Canal and Manchester. On both sides of the moss there are large water flashes, which gives you the impression of being on a large lake when you cross. The boating expression was *crossing the moss*.

The most popular method used by the coal touts for conveying their hard earned fuel home was by bicycle, if you could call it that. It usually consisted of the frame, with two tyre-less wheels attached and nothing else. When a bag of the black stuff had been scrounged, brushed up from the hold of an empty boat, or scraped for all day, on one of the many slag heaps, it was shoved through the frame of the bike and precariously balanced, then pushed home, probably to an eager household awaiting its arrival.

I was being asked by other boat crews, the reason for the captain's absence. I told them he had taken ill.

When it was my turn, to load 50 tonnes of a grade of coal called slack, my two temporary mates assisted me in distributing the five railway wagons over the full length of the hold. This is done by moving the boat slowly forward as the wagons are tipped over on the cradle one at a time allowing the contents to slip out.

A motor boat was usually loaded bow first unlike a dummy or horse drawn boat, the reason for this was because you had to be careful when filling the stern end that as the draught went deeper not to allow the engine exhaust hole to go below the water line.

After the loading of the *Progress* was completed, the slack was trimmed into the shape of a house roof or a tent from stem to stern by my two helpers under my direction and the decks washed off while I navigated her back across the moss to Poolstock locks.

The two Wiganers saw me clear of the remaining locks to Wigan Pier, before taking their leave at Seven Stars Bridge pushing a booty of two bags apiece of the black gold wedged between the frames of their ramshackle bikes. So grateful was I for their help that I gave each of them an empty sack to fill with the compliments of Tate & Lyle!

I was alone once more, and heading for Gathurst and the open country, feeling quite proud of my achievements thus far.

The delivery notes from the colliery were in the cabin, and I wanted to get to Liverpool as quickly as possible to hand them in at the office of Richard Williams & Sons as proof of my prowess.

After negotiating Deane Lock at Gathurst, the penultimate one before the twenty-eight mile stretch of level to Liverpool, I tied the boat to the side in a temporary fashion while I made myself a meal. I was ravishingly hungry, and very tired. It was 2 o'clock in the afternoon, and I'd been on the go for thirteen hours non-stop. While I was eating I was barely able to keep awake, so I decided to have a few hours sleep before continuing.

It was my intention to go down Appley Lock under cover of darkness again, so as not to be observed by Tom and Ann Bowen who I'm sure would not have approved of what I was doing.

All that day I had fully expected someone from the company to come looking for me and their boat I was quite surprised they had not. It seemed as if they hadn't been informed. Perhaps the marooned captain had not yet got over the shock of finding his charge missing?

I had a four-hour sleep at Deane Lock, (the replica of John Constable's The Haywain) and it was now quite dark. I made myself more tea before going aft to start the engine and getting under way again.

I passed down Appley Lock uneventfully, and it was plain sailing, excepting for the wooden bridges that required to be turned off and on but that was a more manageable task, than working single-handed through locks.

One of the runners in the 1948 Grand National did not 'turn' at the Canal Turn!
Jockey Tim Malony looks on.

Taking extra care when steering *Progress* around the half moon turn
at Newburgh ('Newbruf' to boatmen) I passed under Parbold Bridge.

With the weight being carried, it was still a calculated three hour sail
to the Ship Inn at Haskayne. I was planning to pass the captain's house at
about 1 o'clock in the morning anticipating he would be in bed again.It
was now twenty-four hours since I made off with the boat!

It was in fact nearer to 2am when I passed his cottage and everywhere was in total darkness.

By now I had come to realize what an asset the bow headlight was as
its beam shone ahead lighting the way through the narrow bridge holes
where there was a clearance of only 12 inches each side of the boat as
she went under them.

At 5am I made another stop, for one hour, on the long straight stretch
known to boatmen as *Aintree Val*, which runs parallel with the Aintree
Steeplechase Course.

I stopped the engine to allow it to cool, filled the lubricating box with
oil, and made another meal before resuming, to cover the last ten miles
to the sugar refinery.

By 9am I was handing James Lovelady, the operator of the electrically
lifted steel bridge at Litherland, the toll notes, which defined and iden-

The 'Margaret' and 'Progress' at Scarisbrick en route to Liverpool.

tified the cargo, its weight, and the distance carried for calculating the charges due to the Canal Company.

I was now passing through the built-up area of Bootle, with its factories and old houses adjacent to the canal. On the towpath side was the wall of the gasworks with the crane grab perched at the top by the main installations.

Scores of boats belonging to John Parke & Sons were moored alongside the wall. Some were fully laden with different grades of coal, and others had been discharged and ready to be taken back to the Bankhall Sidings for another cargo.

On top of the whole length of the wall was a two foot wide walkway along which the watchman patrolled as far as Litherland Road Bridge, where there was an opening which gave access to and from the public highway, only yards from where I was born. The watchman's job was to walk the wall, especially in the dark, to deter members of the public, armed with all kinds of receptacles, from pilfering coal from the boats. This was a period of mass unemployment in Bootle.

To us *young uns* it was another way of making a copper or two by delivering a bucketful of coal to grateful old people who lived in cold houses, with only ten shillings a week pension, for as little as one penny they would have a fire all night.

It was too much of a temptation to people without fires when there was hundreds of tonnes laying so close by.

My father (aged 66) forced to 'bow haul' 60 tonnes of coal two miles as the horse was indisposed, 1948.

When I reached Chisenhall Street Bridge and the Tate & Lyle factories, I tied the *Progress* for and aft, to the steel rings embedded in the coping stones for that purpose, had a wash and brush up, and set off along Pall Mall to Chapel Street.

I arrived at Richard Williams' office and went straight into a small cubicle specially constructed to cater for the clog-clad bargees, to keep them segregated and out of sight of other general callers better dressed for the city!

After announcing myself I was asked to enter the private office of Mr Arnold Jones, (we employees called him *Dicky Jones* among ourselves).

The first thing he wanted to know was the whereabouts of his boat *Progress*, and was there any damage to her? He seemed relieved, then slightly amused, when I informed him she was tied up at the refinery, safe and sound, and with 50 tonnes of carge waiting to be discharged. To prove the fact I handed him the delivery notes from Garswood Hall Colliery.

Arnold Jones asked me why I'd embarked on such a foolhardy enterprise? I explained to him about the tying up episodes in the middle of the afternoon, etc., which was the reason why my predecessor had left his employ. He became very interested as if he was being enlightened about something he had not hitherto been aware of.

Arnold Jones knew that bargees and boating was not only a trade it was a Romany way of life, replacement of crews was not easy, despite the unemployment in the country.

He also knew that my dad worked the horse boat *Robert Arthur* for him.

After giving him the reasons for doing what I did, he told me I wasn't going to be sacked, but as a result of my actions it was now impracticable for me to continue as mate on the *Progress*.

The proposal

Being a shrewd businessman Dicky Jones put a proposal to me and I don't think it was one he'd just thought up. He said I could have charge of a dummy boat (to be towed behind one of the company's motor boats) engaged in bringing coal from Wigan to Liverpool. The job was not immediately available and I would have to wait a week or two, without pay, while the boat in question was being overhauled at Mayor's boatyard in Wigan Basin.

Dummy boat *Richard* was having her timbers re-caulked with oakum and tarred with black bitumen to make her watertight.

It was a business ploy whereby two boats could be worked by three men, in this instance by two men and a boy, instead of the usual four men and a horse, thus cutting down the wage bill.

Another factor was that the dummy boat being towed had a greater carrying capacity than the motor boat ie, 65 tonnes as against 50 tonnes. It meant over 100 tonnes of cargo being transported in one trip, and tonnage was the object of his business.

I accepted Mr Jones' offer with a half promise from him that when I became eighteen he would consider me to have a motor boat of my own.

With the interview over I left the office after collecting my 30 shillings wages.

I spent the evening in the Burlington Cinema which was sandwiched between the main buildings of the giant Tate & Lyle factories on the corner of Burlington Street and Vauxhall Road. That night I slept aboard the *Progress* for the last time.

The following morning I packed my belongings into a bag and left before captain Jem Webster was due to arrive from his cottage in

One of Bootle Corporation's boats (ordinarily used for transportation of refuse) near Litherland Road Bridge, Williams's Toffee Factory and 'King Dick's' pub, 1944.

Haskayne. I left the keys with the Tate & Lyle grab man as the boat was being discharged.

I caught up with my father and his mate Billy McAlpine and spent the next four weeks being an extra mate. During that period I was to learn at first hand more about my dad's drinking habits and the way he carried on with different women he met in public houses, especially those in the vicinity of Scotland Road.

Mate Billy had been boating on the canal as a mate to different captains for as long as anyone could remember. It was said that he had no relatives whatsoever and had been brought up in an orphanage in the 1870s. Like my father he could neither read nor write. Billy also had the mentality of a ten year old.

He was happy-go-lucky and when he wasn't enjoying a free pipeful of tobacco he was a constant whistler. When I say a free pipeful of tobacco that isn't strictly true; he did not receive any wages from the captains, just a few handouts and his keep, he liked to go to the picture houses when he got the chance and the coppers to pay.

My father had brought him out of the workhouse in Ormskirk where he'd been since another boat captain he had been mate with had died.

Old Billy, having no home to go to, was forced to seek refuge in the institution, as did lots of boatmen when their working days were over.

One evening towards the end of my temporary stay with my father, and when we were en-route into Liverpool, laden with 65 tonnes of coal, he decided to stop and spend the night at the Tailors Arms, on Gorsey Lane Sefton five miles north of Liverpool where there was stabling for the horse at the rear of the pub.

The horse had pulled the 65 tonnes about 18 miles that day mostly against a headwind from Burscough and my dad thought it had done enough for one day.

I took the horse to the stables where I fed and watered him and put clean straw bedding down in his stall before returning to the boat for my tea. When I returned, my father had gone to the pub for his usual pint or two of beer. Billy and I had our tea together without him.

Because of the three of us living aboard the boat Billy had to sleep in the bow cabin on a palliasse of straw while I slept in one of the two bunks in the stern cabin with my dad.

From where we moored it was only a fifteen minute walk down the lane to Litherland where my sister Jane lived, so after tea, I decided to pay her a visit as a way of spending an evening, and to see how she and her two young daughters were getting along on their own, my brother-in-law having been called up into the Royal Navy.

Shock treatment

I returned to the boat about 11pm and clambering down into the cabin I found my father in his bunk with a woman who, I assumed, he had picked up in the pub. With a feeling of disgust and dismay that he would do such a thing while I was working with him, I jumped back up onto the deck again. At first, not knowing what to do, I went to the bow cabin where Billy McAlpine was laying in his bunk and filling the cabin full of smoke from his pipe. I told Billy about the *carry on* in the stern cabin but he made no comment, he couldn't say a lot because he depended on my father to provide him with food and shelter. The alternative was Ormskirk Workhouse.

I did construe from Billy that it wasn't the first time for such occurrences. I sat in the bow cabin fuming for a few minutes until my disgust got the better of my rationality and reasoning.

Jumping back through the scuttle I walked back to the stern cabin, the scuttle lid was only partially in place to allow fresh air to get into

Liverpool Corporation's 'Muck Quay' and incinerator chimney, Chisenhale Street.

the cabin and there was smoke coming from the chimney. I grabbed a sack used for carrying the horses provender to the stable and stuffed it into the top of the chimney preventing the smoke from rising, then I secured the scuttle lid, and applied the locking bar across it sealing the cabin completely. In reality what I was doing was committing murder by carbon poisoning. Had I not relented, the two occupants would have died within minutes.

When my father realized what was happening with the cabin filling up with smoke he started to bang on the inside of the scuttle lid, right away I pulled the sack from out of the chimney, released the scuttle lid, then ran like the wind up an embankment by the bridge that led onto the road.

After climbing some railings, I stopped and turned to see my father standing on the deck in his long johns and shaking his fist at me. He didn't remain on the deck very long because it was a very cold night but as he returned to the cabin he clutched hold of the scuttle lid and threw it into the canal making sure I didn't do the same thing again. I must have given him a good fright.

Half an hour later when it appeared he'd settled down again I ventured down into the bow cabin to spend the rest of the night sitting by the fire while Billy McAlpine snored his head off.

Before he went to sleep he did offer to share his bunk with me, an offer I declined. He was turned seventy and did his fair share of scratching. I was quite content to snooze the hours away stretched out on the hard bench, an experience gained in police cells.

It helps to know a person and their habits and Billy knew my dad. He said to me: 'He'll be alright in'th' morning, when he's sobered up', and he was.

At the break of dawn the following morning my father came to the bow cabin inquiring if I was there and shouted down the scuttle, that he'd left a pot of tea and some toast ready to eat in the other cabin, then he went to the stable to give the horse its breakfast, and put the harness on him. There was no sign of the *old hag* he'd brought aboard the previous night, she'd slung her hook and gone ashore much to my relief.

My father emerged later leading the horse on the towpath, the towline was attached to the hook in the centre of the swingletree across the horse's rear and we proceeded to sail the last few miles to Liverpool.

My father acted as though nothing had happened the previous night although he told Billy and I to keep a lookout for the scuttle lid! There was a tail wind blowing that morning and we found it a mile from where it had been thrown in almost at Litherland.

Chapter Thirteen

My own boat

That week I was notified that the boat *Richard* **was** *off the stocks* **and** had been re-floated at the boatyard ready to be worked.

On our next trip to Wigan I transferred my belongings onto my first command and said 'Goodbye' to my dad and mate Billy as they continued on to Ince Moss for another cargo whilst I waited for the *Farnworth* to come from Liverpool and take me on tow.

Although the *Richard* was only a dummy boat I was quite proud to be the captain of her, it was a couple of weeks off my sixteenth birthday and the Second World War had been underway for four months.

The largest fleet of dummy boats on the canal were owned by John Parke & Sons and were used to keep Liverpool and Bootle gasworks supplied with coal. One peculiarity was the naming of them, all their names ended with the letter 'O', such as *Antonio, Como, Mario, Carlo,* suggesting perhaps an Italian connection.

The Richard Williams' small fleet were simply male and female Christian names, *Fred, Richard, Jeanette, Pamela,* and motor boat *Margaret,* the exceptions were *Progress* and *Farnworth.*

My main function whilst in charge of the Richard, was just steering her when being towed and to seeing she was always moored safely.

The captain and mate of the *Farnworth* helped me to load her at the collieries. Whether they received any extra remuneration for this extra duty I never knew but I don't think so. The only time you might get a bit of extra cash was if you were asked to travel all night with an urgently needed cargo.

I lived aboard *Richard* and my wages were seventeen shillings and sixpence 17/6 (87½p) a week plus twopence for every tonne you carried. There were two hundred and forty pence to the pound in those days.

I had to provide my own cooking untensils and soap, towels, etc., etc. The company supplied the bunk palliasses (which you had to get filled yourself with either straw or chaff from a farmer) and they supplied two blankets, but not the washing of them. We got free coal for the cabin fire from the cargo being left in the hold every time we were discharged at Tate & Lyles.

Coal for the cabin fire, the only means of cooking, was cadged from the coal carrying boats by others who did not carry this commodity. A request for a bucketful of coal from one boat's crew to another as the boats met, was never refused, it was looked upon as almost a right. It was a very cheap commodity in the 1930s and 40s, when a miner's pay was about fifty shillings (£2.50) a week.

Up to and during the 1939-45 war for a boatman there wasn't any holiday or sickness pay nor compensation for undue delays such as the canal freezing over in the winter. If the freeze lasted any length of time like in 1947, you had to go to the nearest Labour Exchange to sign on for benefit and no allowance was made for the fact that you might also have to keep a horse in provender out of what you were given.

Despite all this, some boatmen owned their own boats and plied for hire, or worked under contract, and although they may have been totally illiterate some of them managed to retire or died still at work, leaving large sums of money.

To get it they worked seven days a week for years and today some of their children are reaping the benefits running road haulage businesses.

My father also worked very hard but he helped to make large breweries larger.

Boat horses had to be trained, and my father was a professional trainer, a well trained boat horse could be relied upon to walk the towpath and pull the boat unattended even in the dark, and, like boatmen themselves they knew the canal, a few of its hazards and especially the stopping places and *watering holes*.

My dad would always put a nosebag of provender on the horse at certain spots and the horse would get to know these places, so when it was getting near to one of them it would pull a little bit harder to get there quicker for its feed.

Damage caused by German land mine at Bankhall during air raid, 1941. During the six-week stoppage, many boatmen were forced to sign on at the Employment Exchange.

Nearly all the stabling facilities were situated at the rear of the countless pubs on the canal route and the horses got to know them also. When it came to one of these stables perhaps in the middle of the day, the horse would stop and maybe turn its head to look at you steering the boat as if to say: 'Aren't we stopping here?' Once you persuaded him or her that it was too early in the day to cease work by putting the nosebag on its head they would continue walking and chomping their food at the same time.

Some of the public who walked the towpath, mostly in the summer months for pleasure, when seeing a horse pulling an obvious great weight, thought it cruel, especially after enquiring of you about the tonnage, but it wasn't. To make the boat move, it only required the half-inch cotton tow rope to be kept taut, the weight of the rope itself drew the boat along. A head-on wind did make it harder, but boatmen looked after their charges, which were also their property. The reason was obvious a sick horse, or no horse, meant no work and no earnings. Most barge firms did not supply the horse. I myself have pulled seventy tonnes of coal on my own for two miles from Bankhall Sidings to

Liverpool Gasworks, when the horse was at the smithy either waiting to have new shoes put on him or for some other reasons.

It's a lot harder to pull a heavy cart on the road and that's why big heavy shire horses were used. These types were not used on the canal, they were too big to walk under the narrow bridges. The pulling life of a boat horse was about five years at the most. The constant strain on its back legs resulted after that time in it being unable to to get to its feet after laying down in the stable stall. Some would start to sleep standing up because of this, which meant they were not getting their proper rest. On occasions a block and tackle had to be used in the stall to get them to their feet. It happened to 99% of all the horses and it was a signal that a replacement was required.

The old horse would be taken to the knackers yard and sold for about £1, probably about a tenth of its original value. It was humanely shot and different parts of its anatomy sold to a glue factory (its bones) and the rest for dog meat.

The most frequented knackers yard for boat horses was in Carruthers Street off Vauxhall Road close to the canal and I believe it is still there today.

It was rare for boatmen to call in a vet if the horse wasn't feeling well or if it had sore shoulders caused by pulling and not keeping the inside of its collar free from sweat lather. They were very unhappy with vets because of what they charged. My father always thought he knew more about what was ailing a horse, and its possible cure, than they did.

He placed more value on the opinion of a gypsy having bought a few horses from them in his time. But he had the same opinion about chemists, who he called druggists, and never visited a dentist. When he had a troublesome tooth, he would dig at it with a penknife until it came out. He was turned 75 when a doctor was called in to examine him for the first time in his life. The only cure he hadn't got any answer for was his drunkeness.

I spent the next two years being towed behind *Farnworth*, then in 1942 Richard Williams bought the timber-built boat *Mars* from Canal Transport Ltd and I took over as captain of my first motor boat. I introduced my cousin Billy Prescott to the canal as my mate when he was sixteen.

Billy had been attending a special school in Blackburn because he had difficulty in learning but he took to boating like a duck to water. He and I spent many a night tied up at Tate & Lyle's when German bombs were dropping all around us setting Liverpool docks ablaze from Bootle to Garston and on numerous occasions when we were sailing out in the

Repairing swing bridge at Maghull damaged by bombs, 1941.

country we saw the sky lit up in the distance as Liverpool was being fire bombed.

When an air raid was in progress we sailed without the aid of the bow headlight especially after hearing of one boat's crew being machine gunned one moonlight night by a German plane. Fortunately there was no damage done to either crew or boat although a trail of bullets were seen to hit the water close by.

The attack took place just as the boat *Capricorn* was passing the steeplechase course at Aintree and by the jump known as Canal Turn.

During the war when rationing was introduced boatmen were issued with special ration books. We had to go to the one store in Liverpool to collect our victuals.

You could always identify bargees as they walked into Coopers store in Church Street dressed in their brown corduroy trousers blue gansey, and clattering clogs.

In doing two trips a week between Liverpool and Wigan, we passed up and down Appley Lock on numerous occasions, and at all hours of the day or night. Some times I would tie up just above the lock, and spend the evening with Tom and Ann Bowen in their cottage. We always had plenty to talk about, often referring back to my days in Barnes Home and my escapades.

Ann Bowen was still active and forever baking. When mate Billy and

I departed there was always a large home-baked pie and clean clothes, washed for me by daughter Maggie Spencer, to take with us. In turn I kept them both well supplied with coal and kindling wood. I picked the wood out of the water as we sailed along and, in my spare time after drying it, I chopped it into sticks and bagged it. I then carried it in a wheelbarrow, together with the coal, and emptied it all in Tom Bowen's stable at the rear of the cottages. They always had a stock of a tonne or more in the stall which was once used to house Tom's boat horse.

I spent my Christmas' and most of the Bank Holidays at the lock, and was looked upon as one of the family.

My saddest day

In January 1949 Mrs Bowen died and I lost the best friend I ever had in the whole world. She more than made up for my grandmother Cheetham who died in 1930. One year later almost to the day, Tom Bowen died.

It was said that he pined for his beloved wife Ann from the day she left him, and I know this was true. Ann was seventy-nine and Tom eighty- four. They had been married for over sixty years. They are buried together in the churchyard of Christchurch Douglas which stands half-way up Parbold Hill overlooking Appley Lock.

The River Douglas runs at the bottom of what is a wide valley with Parbold Hill on the one side and Ashurst Beacon on the other.

Sadly, Mrs Bowen's cottages and the Lock Keepers House have since been pulled down. On a recent visit, my first in twenty years, where the cottages once stood, and where I once knocked on one of the doors one dark and wet night as an eleven year old runaway, to ask for a drink of water; all I could make out were the remains of the 3ft high wall that separated the yard in front of the cottages from the canal tow path. The wall can just be seen amongst the 6ft high thistles and weeds. The visit brought back a host of memories and I wished I hadn't gone, tears were in my eyes when I left.

The length of the canal from the bridge to the lock is now a beauty spot much frequented by fishermen.

The only time the lock is operated now is by people from all walks of life boating for pleasure with their cabin cruisers. Gone forever the horse drawn boats, the Fly-Boats, and the characters who worked them.

Mrs Bowen's three grandchildren, the Spencer boys, Horace, Cyril, and Eric, who I used to play with, grew to be tall like their father Jack.

All three joined the Grenadier Guards and went on from small boys born and brought up alongside a remote part of the Leeds and Liverpool Canal, to living in barracks in the heart of London and performing guard duties at Buckingham Palace itself.

Their father Jack Spencer, one time special constable, and my part guardian, died in 1970 aged seventy and is buried in the same grave as Tom and Ann Bowen.

Maggie Spencer, now turned eighty years, is living in retirement in Pemberton, Wigan, close to Eric and Cyril. Her eldest son Horace emigrated to Australia many years ago.

During the time I worked boat *Mars* there occurred an incident which has always remained a mystery.

One day in January 1947 I loaded a cargo of top grade expensive coal called *Shevington Nuts* at Crooke Hall cradle which was on the Liverpool side of Wigan. It was beginning to go dark when we got back to Burscough Bridge and I decided to call it a day, tie up at the Packet House pub and after tea my mate and I would pay a visit to the pictures at the Institute.

With fifty two tonnes in her hold the *Mars* was low in the water and had only an eighteen inch side on her above the water line.

We left the boat about 6.30 and proceeded to walk along Liverpool Road. When the performance was over we called at a chip shop to buy our supper. Arriving back at the boat I was shocked to near panic when I saw that it had settled in the water and had a side of only two inches above the water line. The boat was sinking with very little time left before she went under altogether.

My first thought was that she had sprung a leak in one of her timbers until I saw the lock on the engine house cover was missing. Clambering down into the engine house where there was four inches of water covering the floor, I saw the wooden cover that gave access to the sea-cock floating about. In a flash I realized that someone had broken in while we were away and had opened the sea-cock to let water in and sink her.

After pushing down the handle of the *cock* to stop water gushing in I quickly lit a cartridge and inserted it in to the cylinder head of the engine, then there was the agonizing wait for the dome to heat sufficiently before the engine would start.

Frantically I started to swing the fly-wheel to get the engine powered water pump working. For all I knew it may well have only been the mooring ropes that were holding her afloat, and if they broke under the strain the boat would simply roll over on her side and sink. I breathed a great sigh of relief when the engine shuddered into life.

It took two hours to pump all the water out of the bilge and bring he
back up to her normal level. It had been a near disaster.

Hours later I lay in my bunk contemplating about who would hav
carried out such an act of wanton sabotage. Was it done throug
jealousy? Did someone have a grudge against the two Liverpool lads
Or was it an over zealous criminally minded 'kebber'?

Kebbing

At the loading cradles there was always a certain amount of spillag
whilst loading was in progress. When loading is not in operatio
such as week-ends or holiday times, some boatmen, who didn't cari
cargoes of coal, or others who lived close to the cradle, would salvac
the coal that had spilt into the water with the use of a 'keb'.

A keb is a wire mesh basket attached to a long piece of rope which
thrown into the water and dragged along the canal bed so when it
pulled out again the spilt coal, plus other rubbish, is recovered from th
canal bed, hence the name 'kebber'.

Because I couldn't think of any other reason why someone wanted i
sink boat *Mars* with its cargo of high grade Shevington Nuts, I bega
to wonder if a prospective kebber had done the deed hoping to find
kebbing bonanza the following morning?

After some thought I decided it was pointless to report the incident i
the local police once the engine house floor had dried out, as it woul
fairly quickly with the heat from the engine, there was really no visibl
evidence that anything untoward had occurred apart from the missin
padlock. I intended to report the matter to my employer Arnold Jone
when we got to Liverpool and let him decide on any course of action, h
may perhaps put other boat crews on their guard. There were no mor
such incidents and we never knew who did it.

What I do know, however, is that there was one disappointed persc
the following morning, who instead of seeing a boat keeled over with i
cargo spilt into the canal, only saw an empty berth.

In the middle of the 1950s boatmen began to see the writing on th
wall, that the days of the commercial canal were coming to an end afte
two hundred years. The increased competition from railways, an
lorries carrying heavier loads on the new motorways, canal transpo
was now too slow and uneconomical.

Barge owners began to reduce their fleets and tell boatmen the
services were no longer required after a certain date and to tie the
boats up at boatyards and just walk away from them for good.